WOODLAND WALKS
in the North of England

Webb&Bower

O|S Ordnance Survey

WOODLAND WALKS
in the North of England
Gerald Wilkinson

First published in Great Britain in 1986 by
Webb & Bower (Publishers) Limited,
9 Colleton Crescent, Exeter, Devon EX2 4BY, and
Ordnance Survey,
Romsey Road, Maybush, Southampton S09 4 DH
in association with
Michael Joseph Limited,
27 Wright's Lane, London W8 5SL

Designed by Peter Wrigley

Production by Nick Facer

British Library Cataloguing in Publication Data

Wilkinson, Gerald
  The Ordnance Survey woodland walks in the
  North of England..
  1. Forests and forestry—England, Northern
  2. England, Northern—Description and travel
    Guide-books
  I. Title
  914.27′04858   DA670.N7/
  ISBN 0–86350–061–7

Typeset in Great Britain by Keyspools Limited, Golborne, Lancashire
Printed and bound in Great Britain by Hazell Watson and Viney Limited,
Member of the BPCC Group, Aylesbury, Bucks

TITLE PAGE
Clay Bank: view over the Forestry Commission's trees to
Teesside and Roseberry Topping

Contents

Introduction

As a child I rode the Wall of Death on the sides of a grey slag heap, unaware of course that the shale was millions of years old – or that the heap was a pollution of the landscape. I ran in a jungle of rhododendron, sycamore and beech, without any idea that the trees were either alien or planted there. On bright summer mornings the woods were extravagantly beautiful, even if they *were* in a blighted industrial area. A pond in the middle was enlivened by the flashing colours of a kingfisher: to me it might have been a tropical parrot. I have not seen many kingfishers since, and I was not then aware of my good fortune. The river which flowed by the woods was also colourful – in fact it changed colour practically every day – and perhaps I did suspect that this was not quite as it should be.

Now the river has been cleaned up a bit, but I dare say we should all be better off if there were still a flourishing dye-works upstream and an equally healthy cotton-spinning industry in the vicinity. Birches have spread enough over the older waste tips to allow an oak seedling here and there. The painstakingly neat brickwork of old mine ventilators takes on the surrealist quality of industrial monuments. Some of the slag heaps are flattened, and the cindery fields – which all the same grew crops and harboured the nests of miraculous skylarks – are built over with houses and garages surrounded by white 'ranch style' fences. Nobody ever painted anything white in Lancashire when I was little.

Sad banks where sycamores flourished in the rubbish are being cleaned up, and all – industrial, municipal, marginal, derelict, abandoned *and* natural – is being tidied and 'landscaped', according to some preconceived pattern that has nothing much to do with my Lancashire. In the towns, the same thing is happening to beautiful old cast-iron market halls and blackened corners of Victoriana that will be as sought after as half-timbered cottages in a hundred years' time. I'm afraid it's too late: conservation, by its nature, always

is. The countryside that was mine was full of undesirable things like those great grey tips, miles of railway sidings, decaying pitheads, fences made out of rotton railway sleepers, old, patched up corrugated iron sheds and garages, cinder tracks, worn gritstone setts, sooty, crumbling walls, willow herb, rank grass, adventitious birch trees, ponds full of rusty tins – and, further afield, great empty spaces of derelict land dotted with dangerous-looking 'flashes' and surprisingly varied tall chimneys, some with Gothic detailing. All this has been lost or is being cleared up, along with the pretty tank engines called Hector and Hercules – were they so inefficient? – that shunted on an endless diversity of tracks, great heavy barges of coal sweeping along the contour-hugging canal (pulled by one horse-power), the cheerful midday mill hooters and the seven o'clock busloads of black-faced men. And is an electric milk van with a national trade mark on it really better than a horse-drawn float, straight from the farm with a brown-faced girl and a ladle?

Perhaps we should look at the northern countryside with the eyes of a child, and give into that healthy nostalgia and sentiment so distrusted by the true conservationist. Changes naturally must be made, but nowhere in Britain should the planners tread more carefully than in the industrial 'wasteland'. Now, it seems, even the sour moorlands are a 'threatened habitat'.

Travel a few miles into the hills or up the dales and you will find the richest of country – visually at least – and the most bewitching of woodlands. These are rare, but very convincing, even if they do, nearly all, show signs of interference. Even those most precious ashwoods on limestone are thought by some naturalists to have been planted by farmers needing poles and sticks. All the northern woodlands, until you reach some remote and secret corners of Northumberland, tell a very different story from those of the south-east. Where coal has been available for two centuries we cannot expect to find extensive, well-

Oak and birches colonizing colliery waste, Wigan, Lancashire

managed coppices. Even the (tanbark) industry, which preserved many old oakwoods, died out about a hundred years ago – an oak coppice or two remain in Furness. Woods were cleared, of course, as soon as they ceased to be useful, and an ever-growing population with ever-increasing expectations of decent nourishment saw to it that cattle took over the ground. There are strong communities of people in the North, very strong, but they have not for a long time been concerned with maintaining woods. The older, pre-industrial history, too, is of individual endeavour against hardship and rough weather, and it has been so ever since the Vikings invaded from the North Sea or from their offshore bases in the Isle of Man.

The effects of the landscape in the northern half of England are typical of those of high ground, for this predominates. Temperatures reduce, rain increases, wind exposure is greater, the growing season is shorter. But, above all, the predominantly acid or neutral rocks inhibit drainage. The forest cover must have been almost complete at the climatic best of the Atlantic period about 3000 BC. Trees are known to have grown up to 2000 feet. Blea Tarn (*210 145*, map on page 43), a remote place at 1500 feet, well above the already slightly bleak Watendlath, in 3150 BC, according to the researches of Winifred Pennington (1965), had much hazel, much alder, oak and birch and until the 'Elm

Decline' an equal amount of elm. There were some pines and some ash trees and there were ferns and mosses. It was a forest, or at least a woodland, and though we cannot know how large, it was certainly more than the few scattered birches and thorns we might find there today. The oaks of Ard Crags (page 47) are at about 1200 feet, but they may well have been there since 3000 BC.

Man, it is believed, removed the elms, but the climate was already worsening, bogs spreading, soil leaching out to podzol. Grazing herds prevented the regrowth of trees, as they still do.

The prevailing tree, as everywhere in western Britain, is now the Sitka spruce, but except for some Lakeland places we cannot complain that the State forests have completely changed the landscape. Not, that is, until we travel to the Borders, and here the transformation is surely of desert into productiveness. The bleak Pennine Moors remain untouched and I am sure they should be left in that state, little as I personally like treeless wastes. The oak remains, just, the dominant native tree, but the sycamore, absent until the seventeenth century, is the most obvious tree in Lancashire, with the beech a close second, whatever the statistics say. Perhaps the hawthorn is really the most common of all, but like the hazel it has never been given the status of a tree for counting purposes.

Key

The book is divided into sections which follow on numerically from west to east and south to north of the region. At the beginning of each section the relevant Ordnance Survey Landranger sheet numbers are listed. Each entry is headed with factual information in the form below:

a   b   c

Burrator Forest *568 694*, ♀ ✿, *1000 acres, paths and a forest road, WA*

d   e

a Ordnance Survey National Grid reference – usually of the nearest car park
b Type of woodland: ♀ deciduous
         ✦ coniferous ✿ marsh
c Size of wooded area
d Type of walk
e Owner of site

How to find a grid reference

The reference for Burrator Forest is *568 694*

56 – Can be found in the top and bottom margins of the relevant map sheet (identified at the start of each book section). It is the reference number for one of the grid lines running north/south on the map.

69 – Can be found in the left and right hand margins of the relevant map sheet. It is the reference number for one of the grid lines running east/west on the map.

These numbers locate the bottom left hand corner of the kilometre grid square in which the car park for Burrator Forest appears. The remaining figures of the reference (*568 694*) pinpoint the feature within the grid square to the nearest 100 metres as shown in the diagram below.

The following abbreviations are used:

AONB	Area of outstanding natural beauty
CNT	*County Naturalists' Trust*
CP	Country Park
FC	Forestry Commission
FNR	Forest Nature Reserve
fp	footpath
GLC	Greater London Council
LA	Local Authority
LNR	Local Nature Reserve
MAFF	Ministry of Agriculture Fisheries and Food
NC	Nature Conservancy
NNR	National Nature Reserve
NT	National Trust
NTS	National Trust for Scotland
pf	private forestry
SSSI	Site of Special Scientific Interest
SWT	Scottish Wildlife Trust
WA	Water Authority
WT	Woodland Trust

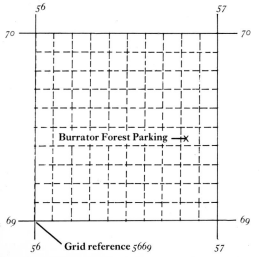

The dotted lines within the square do not appear on the face of the map

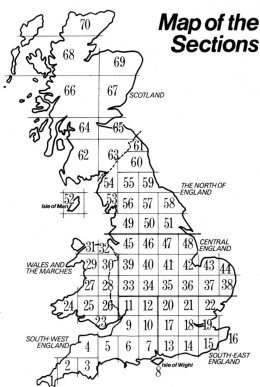

Map of the Sections

1:316,800 maps

RELIEF

Feet	Metres
		·274

Heights in feet above mean sea level

3000	914
2000	610
1400	427
1000	305

Contours at 200ft intervals

600	183
200	61
0	0

To convert feet to metres multiply by 0·3048

TOURIST INFORMATION

✝ Abbey, Cathedral, Priory

𝔪 Ancient monument

🐟 Aquarium

⚔ Camp site

🚐 Caravan site

🏰 Castle

🏚 Cave

🎪 Country park

🎨 Craft centre

✿ Garden

⚑ Golf course or links

🏛 Historic house

ℹ Information centre

🎥 Motor racing

🏛 Museum

❗ Nature or forest trail

🐦 Nature reserve

☆ Other tourist feature

✕ Picnic site

🚂 Preserved railway

🏇 Racecourse

⛷ Skiing

☀ Viewpoint

🦌 Wildlife park

▲ Youth hostel

🐘 Zoo

ROADS Not necessarily rights of way

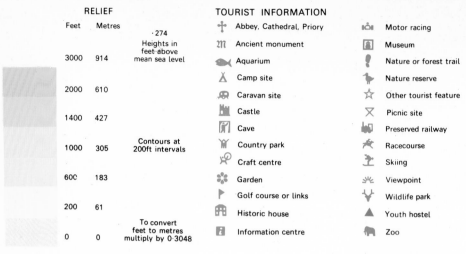

Motorway with service area, service area (limited access) and junction with junction number

M 62   Motorway junction with limited interchange

M 42   Motorway under construction with proposed opening date where known

A 1 (T)   Trunk road with service area

A 15   Dual carriageway   Main road

A 15   Roundabout or multiple level junction

B 676   Secondary road

Road under construction

Toll   Toll   Road tunnel

A 855   B 885   Narrow road with passing places

Other tarred road   Other minor road

Gradient 1 in 7 and steeper

18   23   Distances in miles between markers

The representation on this map of a road is no evidence of the existence of a right of way

GENERAL FEATURES

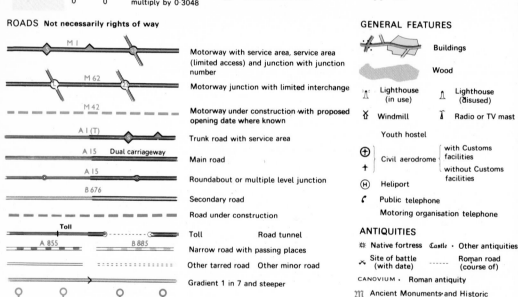

Buildings

Wood

⬩ Lighthouse (in use)   ⬩ Lighthouse (disused)

⬩ Windmill   ⬩ Radio or TV mast

Youth hostel

⊕ Civil aerodrome { with Customs facilities
+ { without Customs facilities

ⓗ Heliport

☎ Public telephone

Motoring organisation telephone

ANTIQUITIES

✳ Native fortress   Castle · Other antiquities

⚔ Site of battle (with date)   ----- Roman road (course of)

CANOVIUM ·   Roman antiquity

𝔪 Ancient Monuments and Historic Buildings in the care of the Secretaries of State for the Environment, for Scotland and for Wales and that are open to the public.

WATER FEATURES

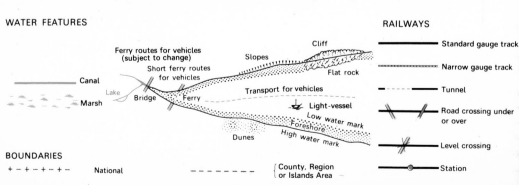

Canal

Lake

Marsh   Bridge   Ferry

Ferry routes for vehicles (subject to change)

Short ferry routes for vehicles

Slopes

Cliff

Flat rock

Transport for vehicles

Light-vessel

Low water mark

Foreshore

High water mark

Dunes

RAILWAYS

━━━ Standard gauge track

┅┅┅ Narrow gauge track

─ ─ ─ Tunnel

╳ Road crossing under or over

╳ Level crossing

━●━ Station

BOUNDARIES

+ — + — + — + —   National

— — — — —   { County, Region or Islands Area

:50,000 maps

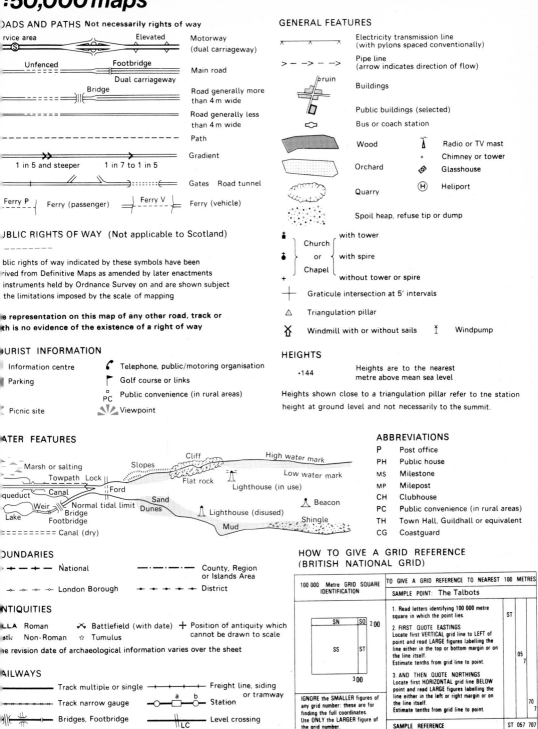

ROADS AND PATHS Not necessarily rights of way

Service area — Elevated — Motorway (dual carriageway)

Unfenced — Footbridge — Dual carriageway — Main road

Bridge — Road generally more than 4 m wide

Road generally less than 4 m wide

Path

Gradient — 1 in 5 and steeper — 1 in 7 to 1 in 5

Gates — Road tunnel

Ferry P — Ferry (passenger) — Ferry V — Ferry (vehicle)

PUBLIC RIGHTS OF WAY (Not applicable to Scotland)

Public rights of way indicated by these symbols have been derived from Definitive Maps as amended by later enactments or instruments held by Ordnance Survey on and are shown subject to the limitations imposed by the scale of mapping

The representation on this map of any other road, track or path is no evidence of the existence of a right of way

TOURIST INFORMATION

Information centre

Parking

Picnic site

Telephone, public/motoring organisation

Golf course or links

Public convenience (in rural areas) PC

Viewpoint

WATER FEATURES

Marsh or salting — Slopes — Cliff — High water mark

Towpath — Lock — Low water mark

Aqueduct — Canal — Ford — Flat rock — Lighthouse (in use)

Weir — Normal tidal limit — Sand — Beacon

Lake — Bridge — Footbridge — Dunes — Lighthouse (disused) — Shingle

Mud

Canal (dry)

BOUNDARIES

National

London Borough

County, Region or Islands Area

District

ANTIQUITIES

VILLA Roman — Battlefield (with date) — Position of antiquity which cannot be drawn to scale

Castle Non-Roman — Tumulus

The revision date of archaeological information varies over the sheet

RAILWAYS

Track multiple or single — Freight line, siding or tramway

Track narrow gauge — Station

Bridges, Footbridge — Level crossing

Tunnel — Embankment

Viaduct — Cutting

GENERAL FEATURES

Electricity transmission line (with pylons spaced conventionally)

Pipe line (arrow indicates direction of flow)

Bruin — Buildings

Public buildings (selected)

Bus or coach station

Wood — Radio or TV mast

Chimney or tower

Orchard — Glasshouse

Quarry — Heliport

Spoil heap, refuse tip or dump

Church or Chapel — with tower / with spire / without tower or spire

Graticule intersection at 5' intervals

Triangulation pillar

Windmill with or without sails — Windpump

HEIGHTS

·144 — Heights are to the nearest metre above mean sea level

Heights shown close to a triangulation pillar refer to the station height at ground level and not necessarily to the summit.

ABBREVIATIONS

P	Post office
PH	Public house
MS	Milestone
MP	Milepost
CH	Clubhouse
PC	Public convenience (in rural areas)
TH	Town Hall, Guildhall or equivalent
CG	Coastguard

HOW TO GIVE A GRID REFERENCE (BRITISH NATIONAL GRID)

100 000 Metre GRID SQUARE IDENTIFICATION	TO GIVE A GRID REFERENCE TO NEAREST 100 METRES		
	SAMPLE POINT: The Talbots		
SN SO 2 00 / SS ST / 3 00	1. Read letters identifying 100 000 metre square in which the point lies.	ST	
	2. FIRST QUOTE EASTINGS Locate first VERTICAL grid line to LEFT of point and read LARGE figures labelling the line either in the top or bottom margin or on the line itself. Estimate tenths from grid line to point.		05 7
	3. AND THEN QUOTE NORTHINGS Locate first HORIZONTAL grid line BELOW point and read LARGE figures labelling the line in the left or right margin or on the line itself. Estimate tenths from grid line to point.		70 7
IGNORE the SMALLER figures of any grid number: these are for finding the full coordinates. Use ONLY the LARGER figure of the grid number.			
EXAMPLE: 2 69 000m	SAMPLE REFERENCE	ST 057 707	
	For local referencing grid letters may be omitted.		

53	56	57
49	50	
32	45	46

Merseyside and South Lancashire

Landranger sheets 102, 103, 108, 109

Formby Point *275 083, (♀) ♣, 472 acres, many paths, NT*

The pines here were first planted in the early part of this century, in the hope that the dunes would become stable enough to allow a promenade to be built. But the coast dunes happily remained wild, only 10 miles from the centre of Liverpool, until acquired by the National Trust. Finding your way through Formby to Freshfield Station is not easy, and there's no help from signposts even at roundabouts. The best advice is to ask the way; or to arrive at Freshfield by train (hourly from Liverpool or Southport). The National Trust parking place is beyond the station.

The dunes are amazingly high, and Scots pine with a few Corsican, and some maritime, cover about two-thirds of the acreage; wooded land to the south and the north is also accessible – as far north as Ainsdale Hills. The Ainsdale woods may be explored only by defined footpaths.

Slacks in the dunes containing fresh water in the winter are the breeding ground of the natterjack toad, extremely rare, and there is a

Evening primrose is naturalized on the pine-clad dunes of Formby Point

section of mature pinewood reserved for the red squirrel, here an imported strain but separated from the competition of the grey squirrel in an island habitat: even built-up areas have their uses.

Poplars, birches, willows and even alders are naturally added to the more settled parts, and I found some oak and many sycamore seedlings under the pine; the humus composed only of sand and pine needles. The sea here comes quite close over the wide sands, but a lady I spoke to would not let her dog swim, as she said the sea was polluted.

Further towards Southport the dunes carry a distinctive scrub of creeping willow and sea buckthorn over hundreds of acres, and golf courses are planted with white poplar. Southport's **Botanical Garden**, *366 186*, has excellent specimen trees in a limited space; *Metasequoias*, an old thorn with large leaves, *Sorbus intermedia* and *torminalis*, a mulberry. The flowerbeds are pure Victoriana, perfect

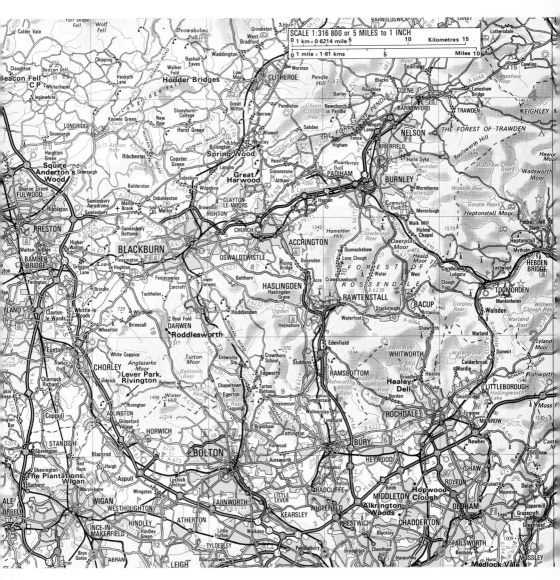

and fiercely coloured, like the cheaper sort of glass paperweight. A feature is a shrubby *Althaea* with exquisitely variegated leaves and flowers like egg cups. There are some sad birds in a row of cages, but you needn't look.

Poplar hawk moth on a Southport street-side

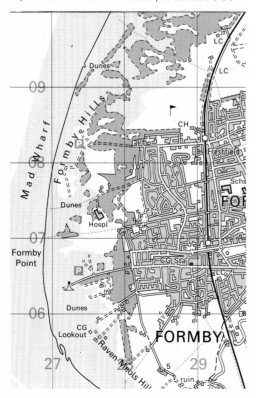

The Plantations, Wigan *592 078*, ♀, *350 acres, various routes and paths, CP*

The map reference takes you to the geographical centre of the complex via a lane from Marylebone. There is a formidable stone-arched entrance gate ¼ mile nearer to Wigan, in Wigan Lane, and a Country Park with its centre at Haigh Hall, *596 087*. The woods are bounded on the west by the River Douglas, whose banks are intermittently lined with old dye-works, maltworks, ironworks, etc. A stream which feeds the river through the woods has banks and bed of a vivid orange mud from deposits of iron, and in former days the river varied in colour from day to day as the dye-works changed its tanks. Roughly parallel to the river is a branch railway, now dismantled, over which the driveway to Haigh Hall crosses by a wide Victorian iron bridge planted with rhododendron, presumably to mask the ugly sight of a railway from the eyes of the carriage-folk. Between the railway and the next parallel interruption, the Leeds–Liverpool canal, are fine, mature beeches; a Victorian plantation which suffers here and there from the Victorian enthusiasm for *Rhododendron ponticum*, an unsuitable and unremovable understorey. The ground is clear, of course, under older beeches. On the west side are ponds, where, long ago, I used to see kingfishers. Beech trunks here are black on one side and bright green with algae on the other, north-east, side. Woodland continues across the canal, a winding belt north-east and uphill to the Hall. To the south-east are old waste-tips from which steam still issues through cracks and which are naturally colonized by birches, which don't mind the warmth.

Iron and coal built the estate (of the Earl of Crawford and Balcarres); the people of Wigan were given the freedom of half of it for fifty years (it was probably old common land anyway). Now they have all of it.

Lever Park, Rivington *635 128*, ♀ ♣, *400 acres, roads and rides, LA*

Rivington Pike is a well-known landmark to the east of the Lancashire Plain – it indicates the first moorlands. On the hillside above the large Rivington Reservoir the Lever Estate was

Smoke, rain and green algae colour a Wigan Plantations beech trunk

given or given back to the people by Lord Leverhulme and has been popular for many years. It is a little untidy and eroded, but has many avenues of mature trees, particularly oaks.

The formal parking place is given as the map reference, but you can in fact park anywhere on the road north to Rivington village, a charming group of houses round a triangular green. The chapel and the church both have remarkable stonework and memorial statues. Anglezarke Reservoir, also with wooded banks, joins on to the north. Other reservoirs, with woodland, are eastwards at Dimple and Entwistle.

The Forest of Rossendale, eastwards, really is woodless except perhaps for cloughs here and there with 'yerth groon' vegetation and sycamores.

Beacon Fell *564 426,* ✦ *, 270 acres, rough fps and rides, CP*

The Fell is an isolated massive hump, up to 1050 feet, covered with Sitka spruce and with a one-way road all the way round at about 800 feet. There are parking places, some large, every few yards. The Information Centre and emergency telephone are $\frac{1}{2}$ mile south-east of the woods at *578 422.* Well-informed people were picking bilberries in July. It was hot, and the twiggy spruce woods slept in the sun. Instead of walking up to the summit, as I should have done, I read a book in the shade. Three hundred thousand people visit here annually, negotiating a maze of small roads which are, however, well signposted, at least from Broughton, north of Preston.

Near Preston is Squire Anderton's Wood, with a woodland trail: *560 337.*

Lancashire beeches green with algae at Rivington

Hodder Bridges *704 393 and 698 412,*
♀ ♣ , 2m of pf by the river

The footpath connects Higher Hodder Bridge,
with pub, to Lower Hodder Bridge, which is
antique and well known for dividing
Lancashire and Yorkshire by a centre stone so
inscribed. The path is on the west or
Lancashire bank, over fields at first, the stony
riverbed cut into shallow steps of the rock
strata. You continue by the back drive of a
château-like building described on the map as
a ruin but now very much restored. There are
spruce woods beyond, then the route settles
down to a riverside walk through and over the
roots of oaks, sycamores, wych elms and
alders: not very exciting and perhaps better in
winter when you can see more. Walking back
by the road seemed to be more interesting in
July, with lovely vetches, bell-flowers, meadow-

Elm by the Hodder

Spruces on Beacon Fell

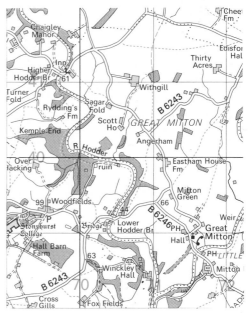

sweet, vigorous grasses and a scent of hay.

The shrub layer of the woods at Higher Hodder Bridge is the snowberry, *Symphoricarpus*, a garden escape here thoroughly naturalized.

Spring Wood *742 363*, ½ *hour walk, LA*
One mile east of Whalley, across the A671, is a decent picnic place in a little wood which could provide a welcome break on a Lancashire journey. Though bathed in road noise it has a charm of its own. It contains the expected sycamores, but they are formidable ones; beech and oak, with birch at the rocky top corner. An alder survives and some larches have been inserted. The birches are greenish rather than silver and the beech trunks seem carved out of the dark rock.

Great Harwood, south of Whalley, has a nature trail at *745 339*; 9½ acres with woodland. At Roddlesworth, *665 215*, off the A675, is a trail in wet woodland controlled by the Water Authority: many ferns, and, they say, kingfishers.

Witton Country Park, an old estate of 130 acres, is near Blackburn: *663 276*. Chorley has its Astley Park, *574 143*.

Ashton-under-Lyne, well inside the Manchester industrial conurbation, has 16 acres of country belonging to the National Trust: Medlock Vale, including Daisy Nook, *922 008*, now part of a Country Park of 50 acres.

Rochdale, north of this, provides its citizens with three nature trails: **Alkrington Woods**, *864 053*, oak, birch and beeches by the river; **Healey Dell**, 102 acres at *883 159*; and **Hopwood Clough**, *878 079*, about 2 miles long.

But you are in a magnificent old industrial landscape – why look for pretty woods? For the real country, head for Burnley and cross to Downham, by Pendle Hill.

Dreary was the prospect on all sides, black moor, bleak fell, straggling forest, intersected with sullen streams as black as ink, with here and there a small tarn, or moss-pool, with waters of the same hue.
WILLIAM HARRISON AINSWORTH

The *Lancashire Witches* is another book I never got beyond the first chapter of. Now, if you go up on the moors at night, you will see the towns spread out like dewy cobwebs, lit from within.

Planted beech and invading sycamore, Spring Wood, Whalley

56	57	58
49	**50**	51
45	46	47

THE NORTH OF ENGLAND
South and West Yorkshire

Landranger sheets 104, 110

SCALE 1:316 800 or 5 MILES to 1 INCH

Cannon Hall, Cawthorne *273 080*
Deffer Wood *267 086, (♀)♣, 200 acres,*
fps, FC

Barnsley is not badly provided with
countryside of a mixed moorland-industrial
character which, while not perhaps conforming
to south-east English ideas of country (any
more than the idiom of local speech conforms),
nonetheless is full of excitement and interest
for those who have eyes to see: abandoned
farms, broken walls of flat stones, old pits of all
sorts full of rubbish, crudely rigged-up gates
and fences; and marvellous views broken by
chimneys and towers. All has been exploited at
random and is beyond repair from a
conservation point of view, except perhaps by
forestry, yet it can be loved for its richness of
texture and pattern.

Down by Denby Dale the country softens,
and large patches of woodland have the quality
of water in the desert. Cawthorne, surrounded
by the old residences of those who turned the
muck into brass, is now a conservation area,
and nearby Cannon Hall, solid and
rectangular, is a museum at the centre of a
well-used Country Park of 24 acres. The large
parking ground takes a number of ten-pence
pieces. It has a new but dungeon-like WC
block and a snack bar that claims to be open
every day, come what may. The parkland is
grand, with beeches, oaks, pines and cedars.
A flock of assorted birds, including both
starlings and swallows, was picking over the
dandelions as I installed myself in the car park
early on a September Saturday morning. By
midday there were perhaps 200 cars.

The shrubbery of Cannon Hall is worth
seeing; beautifully kept flowerbeds and lawns,
nice trees and bushes and charming relics of
local church architecture incorporated.
(Churches tended to be rebuilt in the period of
nineteenth-century prosperity.) The specimen
trees are not perhaps remarkable, but even a
Robinia gladdens the eye here.

North-west from the car park you can find
your way through the rhododendrons and
beside mellow, green walls to the Forestry
Commission's Deffer Wood, across the road.
You can easily park by the roadside if you want
to avoid the car park. The woods are pleasantly

uneven, oak and birch planted with assorted
stands of conifers in the experimental Victorian
manner: try anything. A footpath crosses the
road into the wood, north of the (inhabited)
folly marked on the map. You go by good stony
or gravelled tracks all the way. At the far side
of the wood the footpath continues over the
field and you can turn left by some wind-blown
beeches. Beneath an old oak is a round stone
shelter, strongly built in Cannon Hall style,
classical but with yew-log columns and giving
a nice view over open countryside. Return by a
yew walk and south of the folly by the road.
Here a row of quite large elms has been
removed, every stump sending out a bush of
suckers. Perhaps in 200 years there will be a
row of large Dutch(?) elms again. This is a
walk of about an hour, more varied and
interesting than many which the Forestry
Commission publicizes. Perhaps they feel that
a good bush needs no whine.

Bretton Park *290 131,♀(♣), 94 acres, LA*

Bretton Park, north of Cannon Hall and near

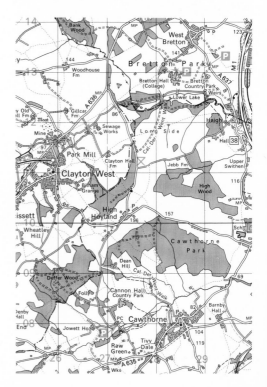

Cannon Hall gardens

the M1, is a Country Park of 94 acres which adjoins a nature reserve surrounding an artificial lake dating from about 1800. Several pleasantly printed leaflets are available at the car park; one of them gives details of three walks. There is mixed woodland and the surrounding farmland is open to the walker. The warden was appealing for 3-foot-high deciduous trees to maintain the stock: phone Bretton 550.

Bracket fungus at Yorkshire Sculpture Park

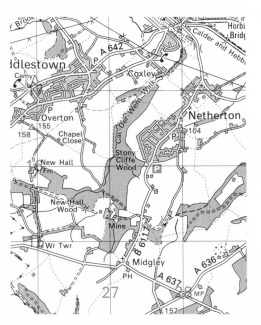

A mile or so north along the A637, parallel to the M1, turn left at a fantastic monument in West Bretton, to the Yorkshire Sculpture Park and Bretton Hall, which is a College of Higher Education specializing in the arts. Terraces, sunken gardens, stables and open woodland are used to display new sculpture along with some remaining, and looking much more at home, from the Hall's heyday. The challenge to the sculptors in an industrial countryside is immense: relics of old grandeurs are all around, magnetizing the eye. Henry Moores look good anywhere, but the 'knife-edge' figure here would have been happier in a wilder landscape. The large group of Hepworths – recently stolen, and recovered from a local scrapyard where they were somewhat undervalued – on a hillside looked like outsize, fake, primitive tourists' goods. Elizabeth Frink's monumental heads were quite wonderful on a formal terrace, while her freer figures on the lawns seemed a bit silly, as did most of the other works, by lesser artists. How a sculptor competes with natural forms is a question I for one would not like to answer with hammer and chisel. I had to sympathize with a wooden crudity; an umbrella apparently made by a woodworker who had never seen such a thing and had got the proportions ludicrously wrong. This did not fit in with anything, but it was at least made of wood and it made me laugh – laughs are rather rare on lonely woodland walks.

Sculpture happenings with smoke and fire, assisted by the Arts Council, had left some charred stumps, while an enterprising *Fish* on the ground, with scales of turd-shaped dirt, had not yet been accidentally stepped on. A few chips might have helped here, or perhaps a giant sauce bottle? Geodesic domes for shelter and vigorously designed bollards for car control seemed somehow more sculptural than the sculptures. I like to think of myself as modernist, but I prefer classical maidens in parks.

Further north, the parking place at *275 159* on the B6117, is **Stony Cliffe Wood**, a nature reserve of 100 acres; an oakwood area adjoining Stocksmoor Common, which is a heath of 30 acres near the road. Another Country Park is

Hetchell Wood: beech sapling and dog's mercury

at **Newmillerdam**, *331 157* – lake and woodlands, 239 acres with fifty honorary wardens(!) – north-east beyond Woolley Edge, which has parking places. (Might be a good place for some fringe sculptures.) More impressive visually than anything else in the area is the Darton Colliery, busy extracting the fossil remains of much earlier woodlands, where nobody walked.

Bradford and Leeds and contiguous conurbations occupy the northern part of the section. There is a nature reserve of 29 acres, **Hetchell Wood**, noted for its insect fauna, *380 422*, near the village of Thorner, north-east of Leeds. Nearby are other attractive woodlands, some open, some private.

This was in fact the last wood I visited in my single-handed survey of British woodland. The November day was dark and damp, and I certainly didn't see any insects. I noted with muted pleasure that the tall beeches were surrounded by saplings, the reddish leaves characteristically held long after the parents were naked. Dog's mercury below was still a good green. It will be all right, this bit of limy woodland, 10 miles from the middle of Leeds. I took my last photograph on the last frame of my last reel of Kodachrome 25 at $\frac{1}{4}$ second, performed a natural function, and left for the south.

The A65 north-west of Leeds via Ilkley leads to Bolton Abbey and Wharfedale (in Section 57) with Grass Wood beyond (56).

THE NORTH OF ENGLAND
Yorkshire, Ouse-Land and Scunthorpe Landranger sheets 105, 111, 112

Broughton Woods *955 100,* ♀ ♠, *many paths and forest roads, pf*
On the Lincolnshire Ridge where Ermine Street (here pronounced 'Er Mine) runs, are old estate beechwoods shielding the inhabitants of Broughton and Brigg from the nasty smoke of Scunthorpe. The beeches are now relics amongst rectangular stands of spruce and larch regularly harvested by clear felling, which gives a pattern of cross-sections along what are still 4 miles of woods, even though the M180 has sliced off the tail at Scawby; once a home of the small-leaved lime.

Normanby Hall is a Country Park of 168 acres north of Scunthorpe, *887 166*; many activities are catered for and there are nature trails and good, old park trees.

Skipwith and **Ricall** *653 374 and 669 377, ♀, paths, roads and tarmac, NR (600 acres) and common land*

Skipwith Common is a wonderful open space with shelter-belts of birch where young oaks breed. It is a good place to blow away a headache. The old airfield is enormous. The Riccall end is ploughed but has a network of roads which I suspect are public rights-of-way. There are lots of good places to park off the narrow road which leads north from the A163, about a mile west of North Duffield. The shelter-belt birches merge gradually into the mostly wet heath woodland of the nature reserve, with good alder buckthorn on the south edge of the reserve. The reserve proper has spaces to park as indicated above, and waymarked paths through sallows on old RAF concrete. Off the path it is usually wet. There are many small meres, very busy with birds: 90 species breed. A small section, surrounded by rusty iron posts, marks with a notice about three sad roots of marsh gentian. Clearly it was naive to mark the site.

Some of the birches are burnt in a well-meant attempt to retain open heath. There are

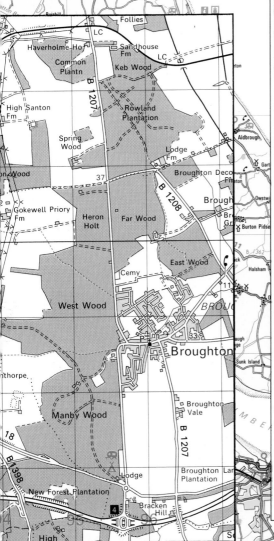

ALDER BUCKTHORN is related to buckthorn but is called *Frangula alnus* – its sometimes rounded leaves resemble the alder's and it sometimes shares the wet habitat. It also grows in old woods. As 'black alder' it produces slow-burning gunpowder for fuses. Its berries are a milder laxative than the buckthorn's – *Rhamnus cathartica*. It is an innocent and pretty small tree, its range not now extending to northern Britain.

patches of beautiful sharp-flowered rush among the grasses. The habitat is described as varied, but this is relative: the general effect to me was remarkably homogeneous – silver birches, white clouds, and little flocks of ducks.

Three miles west of Selby the Forestry

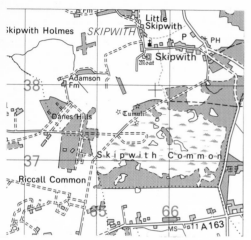

Commission's **Bishop Wood**, 850 acres, occupies an ancient site and is organized to be a wildlife sanctuary entirely open to the public, as well as, of course, producing some timber. The wood was clear-felled in the 1914–18 war and everything in it has grown up since 1921, when the Forestry Commission took over. Poplars are a feature here. All the main commercial conifers are grown, including the grand fir, and native trees can be seen. Patient research might identify some of these with a history of 1000 years in the same place, and since people did not plant trees then, a reasonable link with the original wild woods of what was the marshland of the Vale of York. This is near-fantasy, of course, but worth bearing in mind. There are few other natural links with pre-history, besides woods.

Two car parks are as on the map, at *551 346* and *561 334*. A forest guide booklet, modestly priced, gives general information and a map, scale 1 inch to 350 yards. Walks and trails are detailed on site.

South of York, **Askham Bog**, *573 479*, 105

Skipwith and Riccall Nature Reserve: birches and wet heath

acres, is a nature reserve to be reckoned with, mostly now covered by trees and shrubs. Turn off the A64(T), south of York, as for the racecourse, and park before the railway bridge at the map reference. Cross the golf course to the Bog. There is a causeway.

There is a whole book about the natural history of the Bog: *A Wood in Ascam*, by Fitter and Smith.

Allerthorpe Common 755 480, ♣,
150 acres, woodland walk, FC
The wood has been converted into a poky spruce plantation with a small parking and picnic place. I would rather picnic practically anywhere else around here.

Doncaster: Sandall Beat Wood
609 037, ♀, 200 acres, fp, LA
Featureless but pleasant, beyond the racecourse, this is a good oak and birch wood with little sign of ancientness. There are many well-trodden footpaths and you can drive into the middle if you wish. There is, or was, a Roman road along the eastern margin, but the feature that here holds the attention is a great, slimy pyramid of a slag heap (known elsewhere as a pit tip) with grey drainage channels around it. Along the Roman road is nothing more ancient than rosebay willow-herb (known here as the pit orchid). The wood is bisected by several tracks of railway to a coalmine, with a footbridge over.

Sandala appears in Domesday Book, Yorkshire entry for 'sandy', and beat may

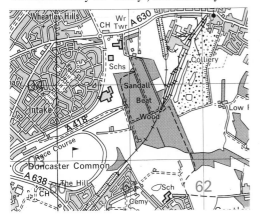

Melton Wood: beech blocks

refer to a 'walk' or a boundary, or perhaps to the extreme flatness of the place.

Melton Wood 516 033, ♀ ♣, 260 acres,
easy roads and paths, car park, FC
Turn off the A630(T) at Warmsworth to Sprotbrough: once a lovely place by the Don, now a little battered – though nothing spoils the almost maritime trim of the waterside. Take the second left through the village towards High Melton, then right at the crossroads to the wood, which has a parking place at the far corner. It is a cheerful, square sort of wood, busy with walkers and riders at weekends, and patterned with a good variety of trees. Some beeches were being thinned to make the brick-like, 2-foot blocks which are used for heavy-duty pit propping, and the blocks were stacked about the rides looking remarkably strange, like Aztec architecture.

Conisborough Castle, by the Don to the south, was the setting for the heavily mediaeval opening chapter of Scott's *Ivanhoe* (I never got beyond the opening chapter). The towpath is tree-lined in places.

There is a small Country Park at **Cusworth Park**, *548 038*, 2 miles east of Melton Wood, the Georgian house now a museum. Of several Forestry Commission plantations around Doncaster, forming the Don Forest, the largest is north-west of Bawtry. It is not accessible – yet – but there is a very pretty oak-birch corner between the road and the railway at the south-east, near to Bawtry, a popular village.

Isle of Man

Landranger sheet 95

No one need be afraid that the island is too small to contain TT races, electric trams, day trippers to Douglas, fairies, and cats without tails. There is space, and there is peace. The number of visitors in fact has slumped since the peak of half a million a year in the 1930s. The government has been able to think in terms of improving the environment, particularly by conservation.

Manx scenery ranges from bleak, but not too enormous, moorlands, mostly government-owned and quite free of restrictions, to sand dunes in the north and fine cliffs in the south. The island is a block of slate, 227 square miles, with granite peaks and corners of sandstone in the west, limestone in the south. A series of miniature woodlands is contained in the National Glens where streams drain the central massif through deep-cut valleys.

Forestry plantations on the moors are nicely irregular in outline and varied in texture, in keeping with the relatively intimate nature of the country. Larch is much used, giving patches of colour amongst the evergreens. Cypresses provide eye-catching edges and windbreaks. Anything, almost, will grow, even cabbage palms, as well as fuschia, in the

hedges. A few native-looking oaks on the western seaboard slopes are severely wind-cut. Manx kippers from Peel are probably no longer smoked over oak chips, but Peel and other small towns are unspoilt. There are no touring caravans. In this respect the Isle of Man is superior to all of Wales, Scotland and Cornwall, each of which it resembles in one way or another.

Seventeen glens are wooded and preserved 'largely in their natural state' by the Manx Forestry Department. All but Tholt-y-Will are easily reached by bus, or by the Manx Electric Tram, and all provide short walks.

Douglas

Molly Quirk's Glen, *405 787*, Onchan, is 5 acres of woodland. Bibaloe Walks is a glade adjoining. (Bus.)

Groudle Glen, *415 786*, 2½ miles from Douglas, is deep and rocky with beech above, larch and pine below. (Tram.)

Laxey Glen Gardens, *432 843*, is 7 miles from Douglas – exotic trees, wooded banks, boating pool, café and the Laxey Wheel of 1854 (made in Wigan). (Bus or tram.)

Port Soderick Glen, *342 728*, 4 miles south of Douglas, is sheltered, with a stream, amusements and shops at the shore end. (Bus.)

Ramsey

Ballure Walk, *457 936*, is on the outskirts of Ramsey near the beach and the second highest Manx mountain, North Barrule. **Ballaglass Glen**, Cornaa, *465 897*, has a waterfall and woods, a stone circle and a nature trail of the Manx Conservation Society. Nearby is Cornaa beach, a favourite cove. (Tram.)

Dhoon Glen, *456 867*, 5 miles from Ramsey,

has 44 acres of wood and a majestic waterfall: good for ferns. Path ⅗ mile, steep, to the sea. (Tram.)

Elfin Glen and Lhergy Frissel, *453 935*, are in Ramsey.

Inland

Tholt-y-Will, *378 890*, is 28 acres in the mountains under Snaefell. A forestry

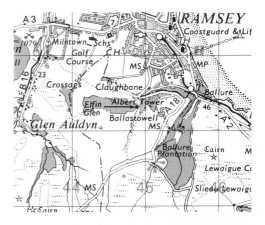

Cooil Dharry trees

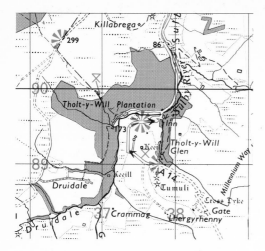

are all close to Kirk Michael on the A3 and reached by the Peel-Ramsey bus. **Cooil Dharry**, *314 902*, opposite Glen Wyllin and just south of Kirk Michael is a 15-acre woodland reserve of the Manx NCT. Mixed deciduous trees include beeches, maples and wych elm, prettily clustered about the stream in something like native woodland – though most of the trees were planted by a Victorian owner. Wooden bridges and steps have been made for a gentle walk of half a mile. A small waterfall is the race of a ruined mill, its iron cogwheels, seemingly hardly worn, lying about in the leaf litter. Neat white cottages below the woods are also attractively clustered in the glen.

Glen Maye, *235 797*, is 3 miles south of Peel, with walkways by a waterfall in woodland which contains Spanish chestnut. By quieter water are banks of Japanese knotweed, a common plant in the western glens. The path continues down to a nice beach. From the road above, northwards, you can see the mountains of Northern Ireland and the Mull of Galloway.

South
Colby Glen, *232 708*, and **Silverdale Glen**, *275 710*, are lesser attractions; the first has spring flowers, the second a children's playground. The Silverdale countryside belongs to the Manx National Trust, most of whose properties are in the south and west: Bradda Head, Spanish Head and Calf of Man, all barren lands, but lovely. There is a deep-sea aquarium on the front at Port Erin, and there was, when I was little, an ancient mariner with a cormorant trained to catch his fish.

Leaflets on the Glens and on the Isle of Man walks are available from the Tourist Board, 13 Victoria Street, Douglas. Several walks described take in various glens. A long-distance path, Millennium Way, is described in a brochure from the Highway and Transport Board, Prospect Hill, Douglas.

plantation adjoins and there are picnic places and viewpoints on the A14 which goes north down Sulby Glen.

Glen Helen, *295 844*, is a large wooded glen with Victorian conifers, oaks and beeches. Path ¾ mile to Rhenass Waterfall. There are a children's playground and other facilities in the Glen.

West Coast
Bishopscourt Glen, **Glen Wyllin** and **Glen Mooar** (with Sproyt Vane – 'white sprout')

Isle of Man, west coast

Silverdale and South Lakeland

SILVERDALE

Like a little bit of Cornwall only with much more to offer per square yard, Silverdale exhibits the conflict of opposing land-use interests in excruciating form. It is not a dale but a series of limestone hills, called silver because they are silver, and enthusiastically hacked and carted away, with bangs and roars, by quarry companies. There is silver in the process, no doubt. One day someone will notice that limestone is a non-renewable resource, its removal leaving something worse than holes under the ground, as with coal. The railway rattles by, hooting with pride at the Victorian engineering skill which carries it across the sands from Grange to Ulverston.

The National Trust is strong here, and it needs to be, surrounded on all sides by wedges of caravans, not to mention gaudy canvas erections with fly sheets, verandas, bow windows and, no doubt, H and C laid on. These are temporary of course, but far from non-renewable.

People live here: hay is made, cattle and sheep are looked after, and all these activities continue in complete peace in a landscape as charming and as intimate as any in Britain, white, soft and craggy. A green and large nature reserve, Leighton Moss, lies east of Silverdale. Arnside Knott and Waterslack Woods are the National Trust lands, and the Trust holds covenants over 50 acres of woods west of Arnside. The most important limestone

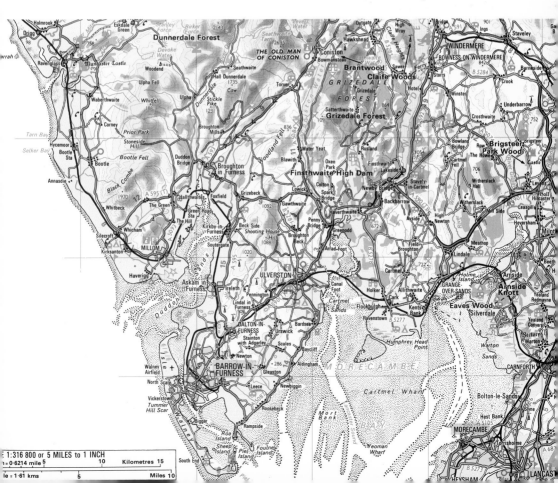

pavement in the area, with scrub, is in the middle of a wood at *480 772*, a National Nature Reserve of 170 acres, called Gait Barrows.

Eaves and Waterslack Woods *471 760*, ♀ ♣ *(yew and Scots pine)*, *100 acres, NT*
Paths are easy but limestone clints and grikes can be dangerous.

After Lancashire's Swelterdales, Flydales and Nettledales, Silverdale is refreshing. By the National Trust car park that Lancashire tree, the sycamore, which was dark green and full of shadows and spiders in the dales, has here much lighter green leaves, flapping delightfully in the wind from the sea. The tree-weed has little chance of advancing far into Eaves Wood – there's far too much going on there already, well established long before the sycamore came to Britain.

Take the right-hand path, less than 100 yards from the gate, and keep on turning right except where a path exits obviously at

Waterslack Farm. The eastern flank of the wooded hill is much more interesting than the west. A line of small-leaved limes, old coppice trees of a wood-bank, may indicate a former dominance – one picturesque stool must be the oldest tree hereabout, although one or two sessile oaks are large. A series of limestone terraces, typically eroded into clints and grikes, contain yew, ash, hazel and wych elm, and there are pines, privet, hawthorn, rowan, holly – and one whitebeam looking suspiciously as if planted to complete a textbook flora, or perhaps it is *Sorbus lancastriensis*.

With the inevitability of the best native woodlands, Eaves Wood is garden-like. Stretches of limestone platform, beautifully patterned by the natural fissures, have the roots of trees married into them as if with affection, yews creep over the stones as well as growing straight up, and there are nice ferns, hart's tongue and spleenwort, and various cranesbills. Privet is common, and there is

A Silverdale hedge with great bellflower

Sycamore leaves by a Lancashire flash

SYCAMORE
First planted in the sixteenth century for supposed Biblical associations it is by now extremely well naturalized. It makes useful windbreaks for hill farms and was planted in Lancashire and Yorkshire for its white timber, made into large rollers for textiles. All the maples are desirable trees, and fine sycamore can reach 100 feet. But the leaves collect aphids and the (strap-leaved) seedlings take root everywhere. In Lancashire the sycamore fills the scars of old industries.

Eaves Wood: wych elm (and ash) rooted in the limestone grikes

much hazel coppice, still cut to preserve the light. Pines obviously were planted some time ago, probably to complete the effect of a natural garden, and this in places they do, their roots particularly well integrated with the rocks, and low branches wandering picturesquely near the ground.

To the north is a fine meadow with shining cranesbill, lady's bedstraw and dropwort, and a view of Arnside Knott, with an outrageous camping site intervening. Beech is common on the west of the hill, including a planted circle of fine, straight, silver-barked trees. Everywhere old walls, floors and boulders are white, shapely and soft with mosses.

There is a nature trail with numbered 'stations': the booklet is available at Silverdale village shops. For **Arnside Knott**, *456 774*, a booklet is in the Arnside shops.

A very small nature reserve, Beach Wood, *452 782*, includes in $1\frac{1}{4}$ acres an amazing variety of plants, not all indigenous, but including many ferns. At Arnside the woods go down to the shore. Unfortunately the sea seems not to come up to the shore very often. Across the sands the Cumbrian hills beckon.

THE SOUTH LAKES

There are scattered remains of oakwoods in the high lakeland fells, enough to suggest that the 30-mile-wide dome of Cumbria was once all woodland up to 1500 feet, with some trees up to 2000 feet. But the valleys of the two large southern lakes, Coniston and Windermere, must always have been densely wooded: they favour trees, being sheltered, moist and too steep for cultivation. The inhabitants have not neglected to improve on nature with beech, spruce, larch, Irish yew, *Sequoiadendron* and even *Calocedrus decurrens*. The Forestry Commission has added large conifer forests on higher ground formerly grazed to semi-desert. These plantations decorate most of the skyline here and descend to the water near Coniston. The whole area is riddled with woodland walks, public footpaths and forest trails. Most are steep: for instance, the footpath from the nice little picnic place at Low Dale, *348 917*, to Satterthwaite, looks like $\frac{3}{4}$ mile on the map but

it climbs at least 300 feet and down again. Of course, this would be regarded as a slight after-dinner stroll by a true fell walker. (A similar distance, from Hampstead Station to the top of the Heath, rises 100 feet.)

I must select, and have largely avoided tracts of conifer plantation and sought after easy walks among native trees. There is no lack of information if you want to scale the heights; the excellent works of A. Wainwright are available at all Lakeland bookshops. Only 3 of the 56 gruelling hikes in his *The Outlying Fells of Lakeland ... for Old Age Pensioners and Others* are in woodland. They range from 2 miles to $11\frac{1}{4}$ miles. His route to the limestone crag of Whitbarrow is partly in woodland and partly in a nature reserve; he describes it as 'beautiful every step of the way': 8 miles. It is only 1 mile from Witherslack Hall, *437 860*, to Lord's Seat on Whitbarrow, though the path ascends 600 feet. Out of respect for this fine craftsman/walker, we reproduce below, by permission, his drawing of part of the Whitbarrow Scar. Whitbarrow, a 250-acre nature reserve, is also known as Hervey Reserve. There are a few ash trees on the clints, rooted, I suppose you would say, in the grikes. (*Grike* does not appear in dictionaries.)

A more heavily wooded limestone pavement is by Hutton Roof, called Lancelot Clark Storth: Pickles Wood adjoins. This nature reserve is of 143 acres at about *546 776* (just off

our map). A good range of lime-loving trees and shrubs may be found here, including some juniper; but note that sycamore cares not where it grows.

Brigsteer Park Wood *488 876*, ♀ ♣
(yews), 150 acres, ¾m bridleway, NT
With oaks and birches over the quiet minor road, several shady places to stop, and mossy limestone walls, this looks like a strip of National Trust wallpaper woodland. It is more: ancient yews surrounded by old coppiced ash stools; lilies of the valley and butterfly orchid. Perhaps the yew and ash were the original vegetation, the oaks planted for usefulness, birch creeping into clearings.

Finsthwaite High Dam *368 883*, ♣, *1m, easy but steep, LA*
A broad path leads up from the decent parking place, through oaks, to the lovely tarns planted with larches, where ducks and geese live in

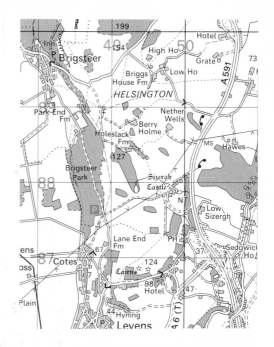

Finsthwaite, lower dam

peace, except on fine sunny days when people dive in. Marsh cinquefoil, with purple-red stars, grows by the lower dam, and there are white water-lilies in the upper tarn.

For a woodland road to Hawkshead from Newby Bridge, go by Rusland, Thwaite Head and Dale Park to the pretty Esthwaite Water. (Turn sharp right when you see the water, for the car park. Here people catch eels at night.) There are several pleasant stopping places on this road, with footpaths and bridleways to right and left. It is worth climbing through fine oaks, up to the spruces where bogs in hollows are full of rushes, myrtle, asphodel and heaths. The midges can be ticklish.

Claife Woods, Windermere *385 995 (Red Nab)*, ♀ ♣, *750 acres, easy or tough according to direction, NT*

It was hot, and I took the easy road along the shore. The National Trust guide describes this as the least spoilt part of Windermere's shores. It is, certainly, a long time since it *was* spoilt by conversion to beech, larch and Douglas fir. The trees are now impressive, even solemn. There are a few oaks and alders near the water. There is no access by car, but this was the noisiest wood I had ever been in, with water skiing and tasteless demonstrations by the RAF. What are the spoilt bits like I wonder . . . but this was a fine Saturday in July. There was

Claife Woods, Windermere: Douglas fir and beech

a good deal of non-biodegradable material on the shore, 1 mile of which is wooded from Belle Grange south. 'Water birds may be seen', says the 1984 *Guide to Britain's Nature Reserves.* Maybe, out of 'season'.

Grizedale Forest *336 945,* ♀ ♠ *, 6000 acres, various walks and nature trails, FC*
Much fine oak and some parkland trees remain around this very civilized Visitors' Centre (the only one I have met with an apostrophe), arranged around the site of a mansion once used to house German officer prisoners, then pulled down. The grand terrace overlooks a lawn now dotted with the latest canvas homes-

from-home, but I guess this is only for two months of the year. The valley floor is flat, and, except for a few decorative drumlins, obviously the bed of a lake, some 150 feet higher than Windermere, which somehow got away or dried up, leaving behind superb farmland. The Forestry Commission runs a shop, with groceries, and there is a pleasant-looking hotel just up the road. I'm afraid I didn't do any of the walks, but I certainly felt the Forestry Commission was falling over backwards to welcome the visitor, and to interest him/her in trees and wildlife.

Working south from Brantwood there are several National Trust woods preserving the local vegetation. There are also several parking places. Climbing 800 feet takes you through 6-foot bracken, old birches, fine, straight oaks, ash, yew, thorn and more bracken, the slope being definitely 1:3. Trying this in the middle of a close, windless heatwave, I was greeted with overwhelming enthusiasm by the resident fly population. Exhausted, I lay down and immediately began to slide. Interesting to see the yews though, and the lake below, still as yoghurt, with blue cardboard hills above. What makes trees, and for that matter bracken, grow vertically I wonder, even on a steep slope? If they had been merely seeking the light it would here take them out at an angle: clearly, from the first shoot, they are gravity-orientated – or star-struck.

Brantwood *313 958,* ♀ *, nature trails, not on Saturdays, pf*
I expected the grounds of Ruskin's house to be full of exotic trees, if only to make the place look more like the Switzerland he so admired, but I was quite wrong. The woodland is pure sessile oak with birches, simple and dignified. I also expected a broad walk, sufficient for three or four abreast (one to talk, three to listen). But I was wrong, Ruskin at Brantwood was a lonely, sad figure, and there is a simple footpath only. I guess this is a Pre-Raphaelite wood; the bracken is low and behaves itself and there is polypody as well. None of the oaks was old enough to date back to Ruskin, and he can't be blamed for the massive rhododendron near

Bog asphodel, Dale Park, Grizedale

Grizedale Forest

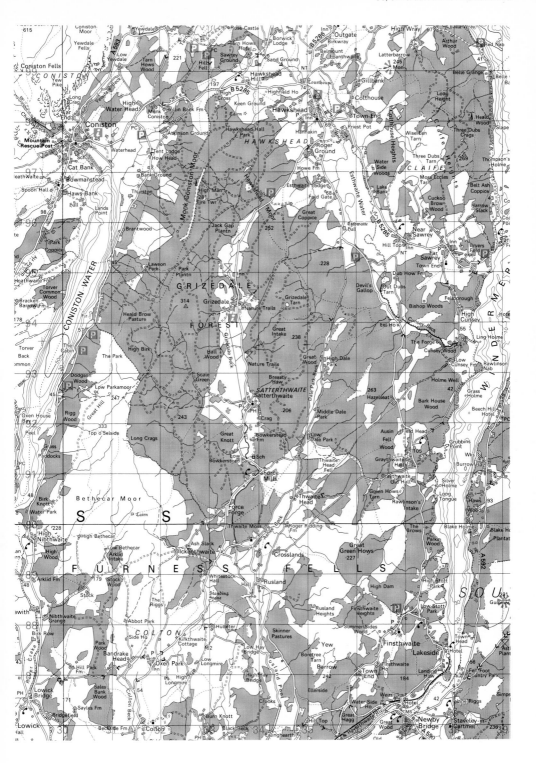

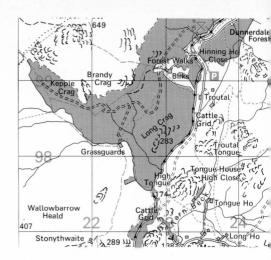

the house; but a patch of large, old coppiced alders gave a clue. It was probably an oak coppice with an alder slade originally, all allowed to grow up for Ruskin to think in, cut during World War I and replanted with oak. The view across the water is entirely satisfactory: he knew about views.

Dunnerdale Forest 234 994, (♀)♣, 1500 acres, 4 walks, FC

Upper Dunnerdale is perfect. Not many things are perfect in this life and I have exceeded my duty in telling you this. The more people know it, the less chance it has of remaining so. The picturesque crags of the upper dale have been carefully planted with spruce by the Commission, no doubt advised by Dame Sylvia Crowe; perhaps too carefully, but they have left a larger than usual fringe of native trees near the picnic place. The Duddon, looking sweet and pure, wanders between marsh spotted orchid, sweetgale, bog asphodel, shrubby sallows. The scent of the gale in the humid air was faintly clinical and wholly pleasant. Here is a beautiful, small, oak-birch

wood with a grassed-over track winding between the rocks: so this is what the original woodland of Dunnerdale was like. Cow wheat grows vigorously. The lichened stems of the sessile oaks are well formed, fine timber that nobody wants: at least, I hope they don't. Near the picnic place the Commission has planted some Norway maples and some cherries.

Upper Dunnerdale

The Cumbrian Lakes

Landranger sheets 89, 90

ESKDALE AND WAST WATER

Irton Pike *120 012*, ♀, *1 hour minimum, moderate, FC*
For a really invigorating view over Wast Water to Great Gable and outwards to Seascale and Windscale this is a very short and easy climb up a forest road shaded by spruces. The Forestry Commission has arranged a secluded series of parking places below the Pike just off the Eskdale Green to Santon Bridge road. Walk down towards Eskdale Green for 100 yards or so to join the forest road. Emerging onto Irton Fell is dramatic. Go left to find a stile for a path through the wood, but this is hard going and hardly worth it since the Fell is higher than the Pike. This is a marvellous place to be on a fine morning.

Irton Road Station on the minuscule Ravenglass and Eskdale Steam Railway (regular service in summer) is handy for Eskdale Green and a walk arranged by the Forestry Commission – called Giggle Valley Walk; $\frac{3}{4}$ mile of larch and beech.

Greengate Wood, Santon Bridge
114 024, ♀, *600 acres, NT*
There are several National Trust woods about Nether Wasdale: this is the finest. It is listed by R. S. R. Fitter in *Finding Wild Flowers* (1971) as an ancient oakwood. I cannot dispute this but found only a few old coppice trees. Mostly it is fine, middle-aged sessile oak, well spaced over grass, or rather grass and honeysuckle which here spreads as a field layer. There is a large larch in the middle, which is rather odd, but also a lovely bog, a really beautiful accretion of mosses and ferns with coppiced alders. By a tumble-down mossy wall is a ruined cherry tree embracing a younger oak – a touching tableau, but sad, for the

Irton Fell

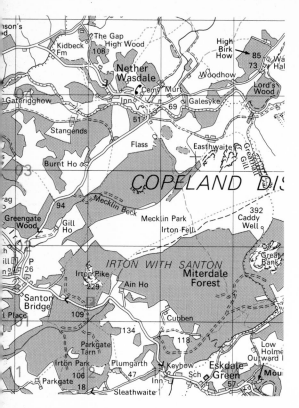

embraced has predictably outlived the embracer. Cow wheat is scattered everywhere, which, with the absence of invading vegetation, does suggest long occupation by the oaks. But there are no ancient trees as such.

Wilkinson's Wood 107 047, ♀ ♠ ♣, 13 acres, no path, NT

Disturbingly, I found this to be a wood almost without trees: like finding one's name on a tombstone. There are five decent oaks, the rest, large trees judging by their stumps, are no more. A great part has been planted with larch, and I find this unacceptable. It would have been better to leave it alone. There is natural regeneration, largely birch of course at first, but plenty of rowan and some oak seedlings. It is all quite satisfactory as scrub, and there is a rich collection of flowers, ferns and rushes, without the need for larches. What business has the National Trust with larches?

I sat on a wide oak stump and wondered, was this the Wilkinson evoked by Wordsworth in one of his ugliest lines:

O spade, with which Wilkinson hath tilled the ground!

Greengate Wood: bog and alder

High Birk How and **Lord's Wood** by
Wasdale Hall, *145 045*, at the foot of the lake
are also National Trust, leased to the YHA.
The lake itself is National Trust, and rightly, if
only for its impressive and vertiginous screes –
rare straight lines in the terrestrial scene. At
Wasdale Head is a small wood called **Fence
Wood**, *183 065*: obviously if it hadn't been
fenced it wouldn't be there: or perhaps it was
used, and preserved, to make fences. But the
truth is stranger: the fields of Wasdale Head
were enclosed as early as the sixteenth century.
The road ends here.

Whitehaven: Castle Park *980 180*, ♀, *town park*

On the cliffside above the busy, dirty,
picturesque port of Whitehaven is a patch of
real secondary woodland, sycamore invaded by
elm with a rich umbelliferous field layer. There
are ancient-looking stone-built ventilators for
the railway tunnel below and the paths here
and there are made with dozens of bricks each
bearing the name WHITEHAVEN. Common limes

dominate the more normal, southern end of the
park. The castle, it appears, is part of the
hospital: perhaps the isolation ward?

ENNERDALE FOREST

Bowness Knott *109 154*, ♠, *forest walks, FC*

Straight lines are again a striking feature of the
fells around Ennerdale, this time edging the
forestry plantations – a landscaping sin, but it
must be admitted that the old drystone walls
often go straight. Too studied a harmonious
effect could look worse. In contrast are many
rows of wind-distorted, grown-up hawthorn
hedges which are a feature of the hill-farming
country by the lakes. These quaint pigmy
avenues, while now useless as hedges, do
provide shade and shelter and frame the views.

Good use is made of larches bordering the
edges of plantations at Bowness Knott, a large,
attractive and well-appointed car park and
picnic place. Ennerdale is the only one of the
large lakes which does not have a motor road

Bowness Knott, Ennerdale, wrapped round with forest green

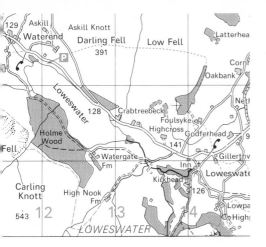

alongside, and the aspect is both green and peaceful. The popular Smithy Beck Trail starts along the forest road – there are two sections, taking one or two hours. The Smithy was a mediaeval iron bloomery using charcoal from the native forest. The industry supported several settlements and, for as long as the soil of the cleared forest remained fertile, there were many farms.

A 9-mile walk also starts here and provides many majestic views. Most of us will be satisfied with one view from the lakeside, which truly is majestic.

LOWESWATER

Holme Wood *122 224*, ♀ (♠), *150 acres, fp, lakeside, NT*

The car park, grassy and with a good view, is about a mile from the wood, but the top of the roadside wall is covered with wonderful greenish patterns of the map lichen, *Rhizocarpon geographicum*, and the walk is also enlivened by meadowsweet, campion, small tortoiseshells and cows, just like a colour plate in a Shell Guide. There are water-lilies and reeds in the lake. The wood is of good oak trees, with ash, elm, and alder by the water, but again there is larch planted. Why is the National Trust so keen on larch? I suppose with 200 properties to care for, it needs lots of timber. But I wish they would grow it elsewhere.

BUTTERMERE AND CRUMMOCK WATER

Scales Wood *175 170 (Buttermere village)* ♀, *100 acres, NR and NT*

The streams from which spout Sour Milk Gill and Scale Force cut their beds in the fells before the glaciers cut this classic U-shaped valley. Perhaps the trees of Scales have been there since the last Ice Age. It is certainly a very appealing wood, much the most original that I have found in the Lake District. On heavy boulder scree covered with moss are dead and living birches sprawling amongst the rocks, while the oaks grow nearly straight, and down to the boggy foot of the slope. This wood

Loweswater and Holme Wood

45

gives every appearance of being undisturbed for a very long time, and this is not surprising considering the steepness and roughness of the ground. It is not really a wood to walk in at all, but one to clamber through, as careful not to disturb anything as not to break your own limbs. These mossy boulders can be very dangerous – and it is a good $\frac{1}{2}$ mile across the lake delta to Buttermere village. There are paths above and below the wood. Sometimes

described as a birchwood, Scales is really an oakwood with a lot of birch as well as rowan and sallow. A straight boundary at about the foot of Buttermere divides it from the coniferized Burtness Wood, where Forestry has reached out its calculating grasp, and taken a slice out of the perfect landscape.

On the village side of the delta a spur of the hillside supports Long Howe, a National Trust oakwood. Howe, from the Old English *hoh*,

Scales Wood

means either a spur of the hill, or, from Old Scandinavian *haugr*, a barrow.

Crummock Water is the artists' lake; it gleams like steel below the variegated peaks to the west, or looks engagingly inky from the fellside. The poets' lake is Derwent Water, and the road between is steep up to Newlands Hause, a National Trust viewpoint over 2000 acres of Trust bracken in the awesome cavity down which flows the Sail Beck, back to Long

Howe. Hause is from *hals*, a neck or ridge, which is true enough; but the Sail, from *sealh* (Old English), sallow, is no longer a willowed beck. Above Kestadale Beck, which flows east, are the **Ard Crags**, *207 194*. Ard is a lovely name which might mean a dwelling place, eagle or gravel, or all three, but which I like to think of as 'ard, the aspirate being hardly worth the breath once you have climbed up there. This is the site of a high-level oakwood of about 30 acres, set at an angle of 45 degrees. Astonishingly at this height and angle it is a small coppice. Imagine the labour of cutting your timber on this slope; getting it home, down the 300-foot slope, would be easy, of course. I was pleased to note the glossy, reddish leaves of new shoots on an apparently dead stump. Oaks in a younger part of the wood to the east are straight, not coppiced: all are sessile.

It used to be thought that the 'stunted' forms of these hillside oaks were the result of exposure, until it was realized that all were once coppiced. This little wood is a remnant of many thousands of acres, converted to arable or pasture, then becoming poor rough pasture or, in better soil, useless bracken. Apart from the many essential uses of small timber the bark was stripped for tanning leather. A local industry was the making of oak swills – woven

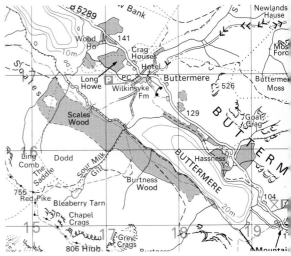

baskets used for carrying practically everything from fish through babies to coal. They are still made, I believe, in Furness.

ABOVE KESWICK

Brandelhow Park *249 200*, ♀ *(♣)*, *80 acres, easy fp, NT*
You can stop your car in the shade here and feed the red squirrels – mine had Weetabix – then wander down easy gradients to the lake shore, which is clean. There is a pretty view of Derwent Water and its wooded islands – two are National Trust lands, but not the nearest, St Herbert's. There, an eccentric owner once built himself a prehistoric stone circle, and

other follies. The woods of Brandelhow are oak, larchified but nice, with springy moss underfoot and plenty of flowers. There is plenty of bracken, too, on the 500-foot slope up to Cat Bells above the road – ready for when someone invents a reaper that will work on a 40-degree slope; and a suitable alcohol-producing plant. Then perhaps the oaks and squirrels of Brandel can spread uphill; or more likely we shall have larches.

On the shores of Brandel
Dance they to the tunes of Handel.

On the east side of the lake are many parking places – a lido effect – but turning up to Watendlath (Old Norse for something) brings

New shoots of oak, Ard Crags

Squirrel eating breakfast, Brandelhow

Brandelhow by Derwent Water

The view from Brandelhow across Derwent Water

you to the beautiful birchwood and oakwood of
Ashness, *270 195*, as well as to Lodore
Cascade. Beyond the tarn (where you can park)
you have to walk to investigate the scattered
birches and oaks of the fellside.

Thornthwaite Forest *210 245, 4000 acres
at least, many trails, FC*
Bassenthwaite is the King of the Lakes,
throned between Skiddaw and Grisedale Pike
and with a a spreading cloak of dark spruce and
fir. Unfortunately he also has the A66(T), at
his side – a good smooth artery, but no asset to
the immediate environment. Turn off at

Braithwaite, very soon after Keswick, going
west, for the Forestry Commission's various
well-maintained car parks and as many as ten
graded forest walks (including those of Dodd
Wood on the opposite side and reached via the
A591). At the Whinlatter Visitors' Centre,
which is a haven of peace after the holiday
lakesides and roads, there is a tape/slide show
and a good bookstall and all is negotiable by
wheelchair.

The coniferous character of these mighty
woodlands is complete: you really could be
anywhere hilly in the north temperate zone.
The effect is severe – no friendly native

Lodore Tarn from Watendlath

sycamores creeping in here, although there is a sycamore plantation, as well as an oak plantation, at Nobel Knott, the picnic place which overlooks the lake. Douglas fir, larch and spruce, particularly spruce, are the main trees, but hemlock and silver fir are used as well.

To complete the circuit: Thirlmere is afforested on either shore and has several places to park, and forest trails, at *308 156* and *315 167* (Helvellyn Gill). The great Ullswater has one important oakwood, **Glencoyne**, *385 185* (National Trust, 189 acres), while

Brothers Water, *404 125*, has more woods than water. If you are tired of woods, Haweswater and Blea Water, each side of High Street, 2400 feet, have none.

Haweswater, a bastard between Mardale and the Manchester Corporation, has no decent stopping places (to avoid pollution), but the **Naddle Forest**, *500 155*, which climbs its south-east shore above the road is ancient oakwood on ground almost too steep to see it properly. Probably a good deal of oakwood went under the water. Parts may be explored on the less steep slope below the dam, without offending; the trees in the valley bottom are domesticated native – clothed in mossy stockings and rough-kneed with lichen.

There are comparatively few distinct nature

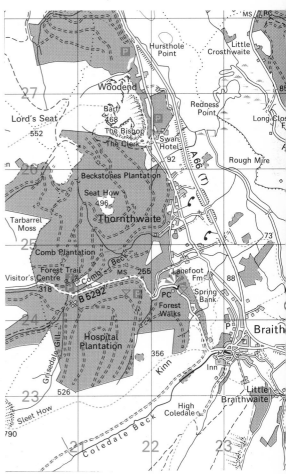

reserves in Cumbria – the whole Lake District National Park is a nature reserve, one hopes. A wood that I like the sound of is Grubbins Wood, 10½ acres, that you can visit by permit from the Cumbria Trust for Nature Conservation, Church Street, Ambleside.

According to the *Guide to Britain's Nature Reserves*, 1984, spindle, buckthorn, wayfaring tree and whitebeam are to be found in an old coppice, on limestone of course. The ground flora is 'outstanding'. What you are not told is where Grubbins Wood is.

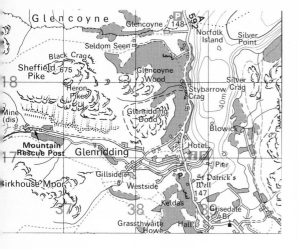

Naddle Forest

Thornthwaite Forest

54 | 60
55 | 59
53 | 56 | 57

THE NORTH OF ENGLAND

Eden

Landranger sheet 91

APPLEBY AND KIRKBY STEPHEN

Lowther Castle has a 'wildlife adventure park' open until October and the road runs through the park, as do various footpaths. You are clearly informed where not to go. The castle is Gothic, and surrounded by fine, mature parkland and woodlands down to the River Lowther.

The Lowther estates have large forests on the far side of the M6: Melkinthorpe Wood and **Whinfell Forest** – perhaps a whinberry fell before being planted. The forest is shapely and a landmark, surrounded by fields on low hills. The road from Cliburn northwards goes through, and two walking routes lead off to the north-west about *585 267*. It is rather dull – strictly practical forestry. But there are mossy drystone walls and other reminders of the old countryside, and one is always conscious of the Pennine massif to the east.

Appleby: Dufton Gill Wood *687 250*, ♀, *25 acres, WT*
Most of the wood has been cleared and replanted, but the Gill is interesting and can be followed south-east to Greenhow. The bed of the stream is of the deep-brown sandstone of which the handsome Dufton village is built. A branch of the Pennine Way leads up to High Cup Nick, 4 miles away, if you have the energy.

Flakebridge Wood can be entered from the Dufton road at *687 237* – a beautiful bit of oak and birch, which soon gives way to conifers. A well-known local walk is from Well House, *698 203*, north out of Appleby and

A Dufton Gill elm

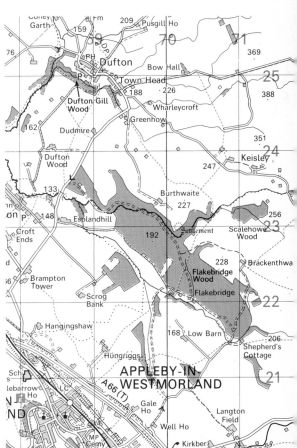

across a Roman road, and then north-east to the wood and left along its edge to an old bobbin mill – birch was the wood for bobbins, now collectors' items – and back down by the mill lane.

Hoff Lunn *657 169*, ♀ ♣ , *400 acres, fp, pf*
Haughr Lundre is, I believe, the Old Norse for

hill copse, and it is a heathy birch coppice which has been largely put under spruce. You can park near the farm, called, less felicitously, Mount Pleasant (and which has a caravan field). Through a gate nearly opposite the farm the path follows the forest road, which is very rough, into the middle of the spruces. It is not an elegant or an interesting walk, until you

Flakebridge Wood, Appleby

reach a glade where the original vegetation remains. Here, insulated from all the world by the acres of spruce, is a completely silent place – perhaps to picnic on the hummocks of hair grass beneath the birches. There is, too, a considerable amount of pretty birchwood at the west border of the wood.

Kirkby Stephen: Smardale Gill Woods *741 082, ♀, 3m of old railway, NR*

From the A685 south-west out of Kirkby Stephen near its junction with the A683 to Sedbergh, follow signposts to Smardale. The low bridge of the old railway before Smardale Hall (Farm) has steps up to the nature reserve. The walk is good along the line itself, but the woodland ½ mile along is only penetrable by enthusiasts: old hazel coppice with ash and birch, some oak, many old hawthorns and (the guide says) small-leaved lime, aspen and spindle. These last three I did not see, but it was rather dark and wet. Melancholy thistle

and broadleaved helleborine were fine and other orchids were many but rather faded in late July. There are 50 breeding bird species also, says the guide: I saw a thrush and a blackbird and some wagtails.

Kirkby Stephen has wooded walks up and down the river. Holiday traffic from the east makes the town busy on summer Saturdays.

A limestone pavement of lunar quality at Asby Scar, *648 103*, quite treeless, defeated my attempts to photograph it at sunset. It is a National Nature Reserve of nearly 400 acres, and, I must admit, more impressive in its way than any wood.

Upper Teesdale National Nature Reserve is very large, 6500 acres, and includes High Force, *882 283*. The complex geology supports many rare plants, including the non-woodland dwarf birch, *Betula nana*, in its only English home, where it has survived since the last ice retreated about 10,000 years ago.

Smardale Gill, old railway walk

54	55	59
53	**56**	57
	49	50

The Forest of Bowland and North-West Yorkshire

Landranger sheets
97, 98, 102, 103

Bowland is traditionally a treeless, or woodless, forest, but it now contains a large plantation on Calder Moor above Dunsop Bridge, and, at its eastern side near the Yorkshire border, the great Gisburn Forest, watershed of the Stocks Reservoir. This is called by the Forestry Commission Bowland Forest. The 14-mile pass from Lancaster to Dunsop Bridge, the Trough of Bowland, is justly famous and not without trees – and at Langden Brook, hot dogs. Here a signed walk to Langden Castle begins promisingly enough in an avenue of trees but is in fact a moorland valley walk. People still 'do the Trough' on foot, but more do it by car.

Trough of Bowland: Tower Lodge
600 539–610 539, ♀ ♣ (Scots pines),
1½m of road and streamside, pf
This is a natural stopping place. It was a lordly

inspiration, about 1900, to plant it with clumps of beeches and pines. Not quite a wood, it is certainly a lovely place, only spoilt by the people who stop to admire it and leave little bundles of white paper all over the ground to show their appreciation. Gulls do their best with anything at all edible, and photographers manage to get the rubbish out of frame.

Gisburn Forest *745 551, ♀ (♣), 3000 acres, forest rides and roads, FC*
The picnic place, Cocklet Hill, at the map reference, leaves nothing to be desired, at least by me. Some people like to sit at a table to eat their sandwiches, and there is a scrap of old oakwood dedicated to that function. As I left it was full of a large Indian family who looked marvellously colourful in the shade. As for walking, you might feel like a flea exploring a rug, but there is a path on the north side of

In the Trough of Bowland

Bottoms Beck to some waterfalls, and a bit of space to park here – just past the Causeway, where the great banks of pine and spruce look their most impressive. If it is hot, you will find it difficult to park in the shade, your butter will melt and your milk go sour. But it can't be like that very often. The Forestry Commission has

left a narrow band of picturesque oak, ash and elder along a part of the road.

There is a fine, old oak coppice, Cragg Wood, in Littledale, with a somewhat exposed picnic place nearby, *546 617*, but the wood is marked private at both ends with new notices.

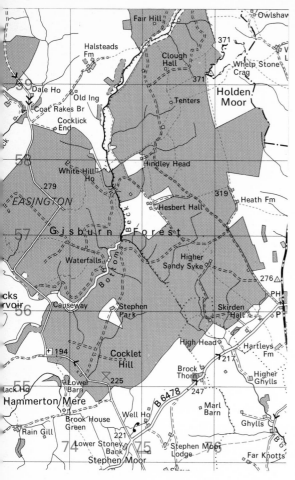

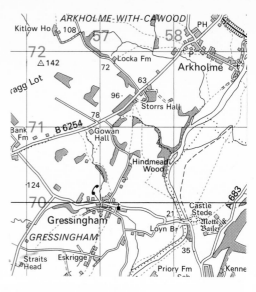

willows, where, with luck, the little wood might spread. The elms are of two sorts, wych elm and hybrid, and there is just a hope that elm disease may not spread further than the few trees so far stricken. The alders are fine trees and there are bluebells and, later, forget-me-nots and the delicately formed wood speedwell, with small balsam covering the floor in places.

Lord's Lot Wood *547 710 and 715,* ♠, *picnic places, FC*
This plantation, a couple of miles north-west from Gressingham, is considerable, but there are no laid-out walks. A forest road crosses to Pedder Potts Reservoir and Kellet Park Wood just south of the first parking place. You can hear the M6, but it doesn't seem to worry the owls.

Grass Wood, Grassington *982 655,* ♀ ♠, *55 acres, steep and sometimes slippery, NR within larger FC wood*
Driving up from Bolton Abbey, Wharfedale changes colour dramatically about Burnsall and Hebden Bridge. Bright green fields are laced with an intricate pattern of limestone walls which look chalky without being actually white. The pattern continues to touristy Grassington, grievously destroyed in places by

My attempt to find accessible woodland by the Rivers Roeburn and Hindburn failed, and cattle flies attempted to poison me – a most unpleasant summer evening.

Hindmead Wood, Lune Valley *581 697,* ♀, *¾m, easy, fp*
The footpath, to Arkholme, is marked near the elegant old Loyn Bridge which takes the road from Hornby to Gressingham. The wood is just a few beeches, oaks, sycamores, alders, and, not least, elms, on the steep pasture where the Lune has cut into the hillside. There are characteristic wide beaches of round pebbles and an island, at present colonized by treacle mustard, Japanese knotweed, Himalayan balsam and monkey flower, with one or two

Oak in Cragg Wood, Littledale

The Lune from Hindmead Wood

semi-detached houses. Roofs of barns still have the Wharfedale tawny gold.

Take the Kettlewell minor road from Grassington on the east side of the river – Grass Wood is about a mile along this road. Opposite the Forestry Commission car park a ladder stile leads to open oakwood – a wood-pasture – between the road and the river. On the hillside, paths lead up from the car park to a natural terrace of limestone roughly parallel to the river. Here, in what is technically an ashwood on mountain limestone, you may find a great variety of smaller trees such as are rarely found in northern England. Whitebeam, not common, is very visible growing out of the rock face, and there is a lot of very attractive burnet rose. Lily of the valley leaves are strewn among the fissures of the rocks and there is buckthorn and much guelder rose in pockets of deeper soil. Privet grows to almost tree proportions. Ash springs up everywhere and is threatened in places by maturing sycamores.

Wharfedale from Grass Wood

Rock rose and bloody cranesbill grow, and herb Robert. A common flower in the late summer is the devil's bit scabious.

The paths at each end of the terrace (which make a very slippery walk, so take care) lead up to Fort Gregory, a ring of stones at the highest point of the wood. Below the fort is a viewpoint looking down Wharfedale and revealing various quarry workings in the hills. On the north side, bearing left takes you into Forestry Commission spruce plantations. Various marker posts with letters are of use mainly in guiding you back to base, but posts B and C are on the route to Fort Gregory. Going uphill at post A, turn right for the terrace.

Within the National Park, **Colt Park Wood** *779 774* is a National Nature Reserve of 21 acres, a strip of now rare, high (1100 ft) ashwood on the limestone of Ingleborough: by permit only. **Ling Gill** *803 785* is a ravine birch and ashwood with a rich limestone flora beneath, also by permit only.

Malham Tarn has a Field Centre of the Field Studies Council, surrounded by oakwood, on its north bank. From Malham village, *900 625*, through Malham Cove to the Tarn and to Gardale Scar is National Trust land, over 3000 acres, and as such readily accessible. Malham Tarn is well worth seeing, even if a lot of other people have the same idea.

Above Wensleydale, south-east of Bainbridge, the National Trust owns 288 acres of **Scar Top**, *959 892*, with a view of the whole dale.

RIGHT: burnet rosehips, Grass Wood

Wharfedale and the Vale of York

Landranger sheets 99, 104

Bolton Abbey: *riverside 077 552 and* **Strid Woodlands** *059 563 ♀ (♠), various walks, easy but steep, pf (Chatsworth Estate)*

Bolton Abbey is not just a pretty place, but an industry. The nearest village down the Wharfe, Addingham, which sounds as if in Surrey, is black and narrow. It has a sophisticated furniture and antique trade, a pottery (Helyg), producing fine craft stoneware, a lacemakers' shop (Seba) and good local produce. (This is the only book on woodlands which tells you where to buy a crochet hook.)

The very large riverside parking field with a view of the Abbey and some symbolic sheep is relatively expensive (though climbing the hill across the river I got my money's worth in mushrooms). The Gothic tracery of the ruined windows glittered inimitably against a misty sun; the set piece all cushioned in rich oaks.

A mile and a half upstream is the capacious parking place for the Strid, less expensive, with a nature trail, also chargeable, but no one tried. 'Geological interest' is the term (on the notice describing half-a-dozen walks) for the beautifully water-sculptured, brown rocks of the stream, where it narrows to the width of the daring Strid. The trail starts in a grove of yews, and there is a legend that the monkish builders of the Abbey lived under the native yews when they arrived from the south.

In the steep valley everything chimes in; tawny Yorkshire fog grass, reddening rowan and the twisted oak leaning over the brown river and rocks: it is probably just as pretty at any season. There are nice beeches at the Strid itself.

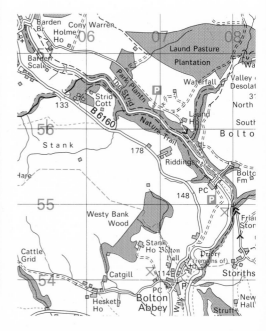

Bolton Abbey and the Wharfe

HARROGATE

Harlow Car Gardens, *283 539*, the northern Wisley (Northern Horticultural Society) is about 60 acres, more than half of which is woodland: birchwood, oakwood, young arboretum with *Sorbus* collection, streamside garden with swamp cypress and woolly willow, and in fact a very good collection of trees chosen for what their bark, flowers or foliage can do for the gardener. The woodlands contain a classical portico from the Spa Rooms 'unaccountably demolished in 1939', says the pretty booklet. No dogs but guide dogs; open

every day until 7.0 pm or winter sunset; charge for non-members.

Across Crag Lane the **Valley Gardens and Pinewoods** bravely offer a nature trail with a good cross-section of native trees in a narrow space between sprawling legs of suburbia. The ground finally narrows to a point at the (1804) Royal Pump Room Museum, so this could be a walk out of the town fortified by a taste of the waters from what was once called the Stinking Spaw. The booklet, however, comes from the Information Bureau on Parliament Street, or from the Tennis Pavilion in the middle of the gardens, in holiday times. It is informative but has an irritating upside-down map.

From Harrogate Tourist Information Office, Royal Baths, you can get a comprehensive series of Dales walks leaflets at modest prices.

North of Otley are Forestry Commission car parks on a forested part of Lindley Moor and near Norwood Hall – in beeches on a hilltop – with many footpaths: *236 530* and *209 509*. In the Nidd Valley woodlands, also part of the Forestry Commission's somewhat theoretical Knaresborough Forest, is a picnic place at Scotton Wood, about *333 585*, 1½ miles north-

The Strid

west of Knaresborough on the B6165.

North-north-east of Wetherby at
Cowthorpe near the Nidd is one of the oldest
oaks in Britain. It was mentioned by John
Evelyn as ancient in 1662 and was drawn,
rather accurately, by Turner in 1815. Now it is
a sad old ruin, but, somehow, I did not regret
going to see it.

Ripon has a nature trail at **Quarry Moor**,
311 692. A quarry used as a rubbish tip then
covered with alien topsoil provides some
unexpected variety in an essentially limestone
area. A small wood is part of the site, which is

bordered by Swedish whitebeams and other
planted trees.

THE DALES NATIONAL PARK

Nidderdale, Wensleydale and their tributary
dales lead in to the Yorkshire Dales National
Park, our third largest. James Fisher waxes
lyrical in the taut columns of his *Nature
Lovers' Atlas*: 'A mosaic of limestone crags,
gorges, sweeping moorland gouged by the Ice
Ages ice, hidden woodlands; loved alike by
farmers, adventurous potholers, tender artists
and dedicated naturalists . . . . The scenery is
consistently moving.' I am afraid you will have
to seek out those hidden woodlands without
my help; although I did look at **North Wood**
on Grimes Gill, *155 786*, and **Birk Gill Wood**,
140 815. The first is out of reach, but its
serene beauty may be admired from the road
bridge: it is on Water Authority land. The
second, on the Swinton Estate, is attractive and
of great interest. A level, grassy stopping place
by the Gill is inviting, though unfortunately
the footpath is fenced off half a mile upstream
and walking is thus limited. In that half mile
the oaks are as natural and beautiful as you
may hope to find, with a white drystone wall
completing the pattern of the lichens on the
bark. There are no birches now by Birk Gill,
unless at the top of the wood, which I judged
was out of bounds. In the valley, all the oaks
are sessile (and superbly coloured in autumn),
but exposed on the hillside of the north bank is
a single pedunculate oak some years older than
those in the wood. Was this tree planted, or has
it survived from a larger woodland long ago
cleared? There is no doubt that the sessile oak
is the expected species here, along with the ash,
which is frequent by the roadsides.

Jervaulx, the Abbey and Park beside the Ure
meandering in lower Wensleydale, gives its
name to a Forestry Commission complex
which reaches up to the Stang in our Section
59 and down to Masham, with nothing much
in between. There is a roadside picnic place on
the A6108 at Ellington Firth, *193 843*, and one
at Druid's Plantation, by a curious, ugly rock
'reconstruction' on a hilltop. A short walk here
is waymarked and gives a good view back to

Birk Gill Wood

Leighton Reservoir and Masham Moor.

On the east border of our section the North York Moors project woodland at Over Silton and at Mount Grace Priory, which is National Trust and perhaps the most approachable of the Yorkshire monastery ruins – but architecturally dull and with a backdrop by the Forestry Commission. The Trust owns 257 acres of moorland from Osmotherley to Whorlton, with the Cleveland Way through the middle. This is fine country, not too bleak, with good places to park. Driving down into Swainby, just off our map, you may see a classic hazel coppice.

LEFT: looking back to Leighton Reservoir from the Druid's Plantation

THE NORTH OF ENGLAND
North York Moors

Landranger sheets 100, 101, 105, 106

EAST OF PICKERING

Dalby Forest *856 873 (Low Dalby Visitor Centre)*, ⚲, *forest drive and many walks, FC*
South of Fylingdales High Moor the map is complicated by many dales, holes, ghylls, riggs (ridges), the dales often dividing at grains (groyns). Numerous nabs (knobs) and knoddles project from the riggs, and knowles (knolls) and toppings stick up at any level where harder Jurassic Sandstone stands among softer Jurassic Limestone, for what geological reason I cannot discover – islands in the warm Jurassic Sea? Scars (scarps, from the Norse *skarv* for a line of rocks) reveal a geology too complicated for me. Many trods (Norse *tra*, tread), causeys (causeways) and sprunts (some sort of steep road) survive from early occupation by man. At Star Carr (Old Norse *kjarr*, marshy woodland) near Flixton, south of

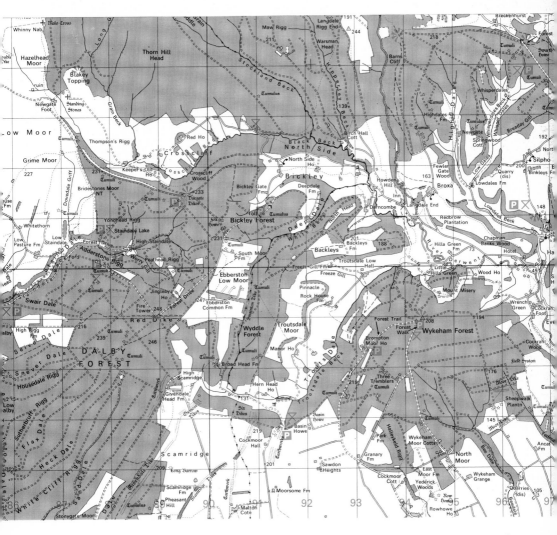

Scarborough, was found a tool made from an elk antler, 10,000 years old. Star Carr, now inland, was then a coastal settlement, but is evidence of very early occupation. The hills were covered in woodland of oak, alder, birch, hazel, elm and pine, and clearing did not begin until some 5000 years ago in the New Stone Age. Excavations of New Stone Age burial mounds reveal the remains of forests below and of infertile podzol above (*podzol*, Russian for ash, describes the grey, leached soil of heathland and spruce forests). The Stone Age settlers would move on, once the humus-rich forest soil was exhausted, and moorland would ensue as beasts were grazed over the old sites.

The Forest of Pickering was a royal hunting ground, ceded by Henry III to his son Crouchback and thence to the Duchy of Lancaster. The deer had all gone by the seventeenth century, while sheep farming, long established by the monks of Rievaulx and other monasteries to the west, gradually took over the moorland. There were large rabbit warrens, where the rabbits were trapped by driving or luring them into brick-lined pits: a ghastly pie, but better than going hungry.

All this information comes from the Forestry Commission guide, *North Yorkshire Forests.*

By 1920 the Forestry Commission began to return the Dalby Moors to woodland. At first conifers were grown with difficulty on the tops, until in 1943 a giant plough was designed and built in Kirkby Moorside. Existing scrub and woodland were used to nurse up some plantations, and was then removed. Now the forest, still only supplying a fraction of Yorkshire's pit props, lies over the riggs like an unevenly woven overcoat, contrasted with the prettily tree-vested, sheltered dales.

Bridestones Moor 880 904, ♀ ♣ *(and rocks), 1¼ hours, easy FC, NT, NR (500 acres)*

Thornton Dale, the attractive village 2 miles east of Pickering, is the gateway to the Dalby Forest. To reach what must be the nucleus, and certainly is a good introduction to the terrain, Bridestones Moor, you have to pay the toll for the Forestry Commission's Forest Drive.

What you do if you have no 50-pence pieces I leave to your imagination. Three miles from the information point at Low Dalby, via Snever Dale, Seive Dale and Swair Dale, you arrive at Stain Dale Lake picnic area, one of the nicer parking places on the route. A notice-board map clarifies the route to the

Bridestones, which are prominent nabs, Jurassic vol-au-vents of perhaps 200 tons apiece made by the great Pastry Cook 150 million years ago by what process I know not, nor do any of the reference books enlighten me: 'passage beds', according to the *Nature Reserves Handbook*. Upland heath surrounds the stones, but the distant views are of forest ridges, while birch spreads over the bracken and heather. Sessile oakwood has remained in parts of the valley of Stain Dale and great plantations there of Douglas firs are already clear-felled. I liked the Bridestones very much – there are nine or so, dominated by the not-

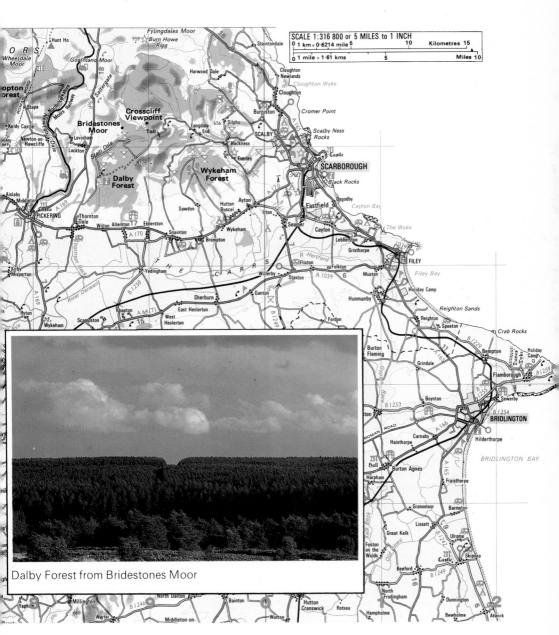

Dalby Forest from Bridestones Moor

The walk to the Bridestones

The Bridestones

Stain Dale

so-romantically named Pepper Pot and Salt Cellar. Sculptors please study. (There are other Bridestones in the moorland area. 'Bride' probably means proud.)

Crosscliff Viewpoint *894 915*
This can be a 3-mile 'exciting' walk according to the leaflet, but it doesn't say where you start. (This leaflet is about the worst Forestry Commission production I have come across, very crude and vague in four awful colours and exorbitantly priced.) In fact you can drive to within ten minutes' walk of the viewpoint by a loop of the Forest Drive. It is worth visiting and there is an information board drawing to explain the scenery, which includes Blakey Topping, Fylingdales radar station and a prehistoric site on the ridge, with deciduous woodland and pastures below, all spread before you.

There are eight other walks starting from different points on the Forest Drive. The toll is justified for 9 miles of well-kept forest road (though if a fair proportion of the 100,000-plus claimed annual visitors to the North Yorkshire Forest actually paid, the toll could be reduced). To avoid being sucked into the environs of Scarborough, on leaving the Forest Drive continue for 3 miles and take the second left at Langdale End for Broxa, where a semi-official ('permitted use') forest drive continues north and then east into the Broxa Forest – miles of spruces, larches and pines – to join a straight, minor road through the trees and parallel to the A171. There are many places to park and there is access here to Whisperdale.

If, instead, you continue straight on at Langdale End you descend by the overrated Forge Valley (sycamore and monk's rhubarb) to West Ayton, on the Scarborough to Pickering road, the A170. The Forge Valley Woods are, however, a 90-acre National Nature Reserve, so I suppose I should have looked beyond the immediate roadside trees.

At Wykeham, the next village towards Pickering, you can enter the **Wykeham Forest**, 3000-odd acres with three easy forest trails giving views over Trouts Dale, *933 885*.

WEST OF THE PICKERING TO WHITBY ROAD

The enormous (about 16 square miles) Cropton Forest, slightly forbidding around Stape, with names like High Muffles, Low Over Blow and Gale Hill Rigg, is less visitor-orientated and less cosy than the Dalby Forest with its many small dales. Newton Dale, which forms the steep, eastern side of the Cropton Forest, contains the romantic North Yorkshire Moors Railway and some rich valley oakwoods. From Thornton Dale you need endure the A169 northwards for only ½ mile before turning off left for Lockton and Levisham – a tremendous view as you descend to Levisham Station.

Cropton Forest Drive and Walks
817 911 to 797 943, ♀, *FC*
The drive from Levisham Station up through 5 miles of forest to Mauley Cross, north of Stape, is not now a toll road – a notice indicates 'permitted use'. The picnic place 1 mile north

Mauley Cross, Cropton Forest

of the start, at Raindale Mill, is on a superb, wide grassy bank and there is a short easy walk across Raindale Beck. There is another stopping place, with a view, near the uncomfortably named Raper's Farm, and a walk to Needle Point begins $3\frac{1}{2}$ miles along the forest drive, nearly at its highest point. Here the spruces are tall and the dark floor is scattered, in September, with gleaming, golden fungi presumed to be members of the chanterelle family. At the Mauley Cross – a touchingly featureless, brown monolith – an Interpretive Trail is listed by the Forestry Commission, but I'm afraid I missed it in the drizzle. Larches border the road north and south of Stape.

At Keldy Castle are tasteful Forestry Commission 'cabins' to let: a very quiet holiday village deep in the forest. Equally quiet is the picnic spot by the Keldy Bridge, *777 908*. Richly growing oak and birch fill the valley.

The North York Moors National Park Committee maintains a nature reserve in Farndale, *666 974*, 1500 acres, for the daffodils.

We have so far explored only a quarter of what might be one lobe of the brain-shaped dome of the complex North York Moors National Park, and there are many declivities left undescribed. Local guidebooks, including the Forestry Commission's handbook, tend to emphasize driving. The visitor would be wise to attempt not to range too far, but to concentrate on a relatively small section. Longer walks naturally take in a good deal of moorland and this may be a good place to mention the 16-mile 'Blue Man' walk from Reasty Bank, *965 945*, to Allerston, *878 829*.

FROM HELMSLEY

Sutton Bank *516 831*, ⚲ ⚘, *display, walks, viewpoints, NPA*
Between Thirsk and Helmsley and at the top of the cliff is the Park Information Centre, manned during business hours and nicely designed in a patch of birch heath. Very good sunsets can be watched from here: while I was doing just that my tape recorder was stolen from my car: be warned!

Garbutt Wood, *505 835*, is a 60-acre nature reserve above and around the pretty Lake Gormire immediately north-west of the car park: woodland is largely scrubby with birch the dominant tree of the area. Heath continues on the surprisingly level top of the very steep, high, Whitestone Cliff, of sandstone, which rises to a thousand feet. There is a continuous path along the cliff edge, part of the Cleveland Way, and fragments of the ancient Cleve Dyke run parallel, north of Sutton Bank, while southwards is a wide green drove road, now probably obscured by conifers. South of the Sutton Bank Centre are three other parking places at the White Horse of Kilburn (Victorian, turf-cut, 300 feet long). A nature trail leaflet and a White Horse Walk leaflet are available at the centre, if it is open. Follow the road marked Yorkshire Gliding Club, east of Sutton Bank for a Forestry Commission White Horse Walk, *514 813*, including some coniferous woodland.

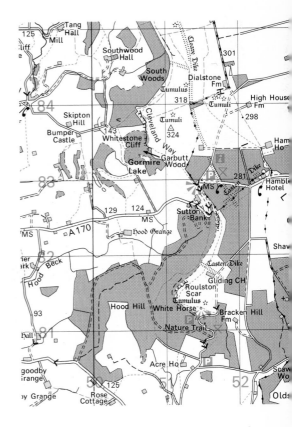

Sunset from Sutton Bank (Kodachrome after J.M.W. Turner)

Rievaulx

The ruin of the twelfth-century Cistercian Abbey, where thirty years ago you could simply stop and stride over the lawns, is now sequestered and provided with a ticket office – as are most important ruins of course, but here the giant fossil seems ignominiously exhibited as in a booth at a fair. You can see the building from the National Trust **Rievaulx Terrace**, approached above the village. These 60 acres, heavily wooded, were bought by the National Trust after an appeal in 1972. The map reference is *579 848*, but note that even the National Park Visitors' Handbook (from the Information Service at Helmsley) advises avoiding the place on bank holidays. A walk to Rievaulx, $3\frac{1}{2}$ miles, is signposted from Helmsley.

Newgate Bank *564 890*, ♀, *viewpoint, FC*
The B1257, Malton to Stokesley, is a favourite road of mine, now becoming rather busy with tankers and heavy lorries. Three miles north of Helmsley the Forestry Commission has arranged a splendid large car park using the conifers as walls to back up a viewpoint looking wide over Bilsdale. The breadth and clarity of the whole are in decided contrast with the claustrophobic Rievaulx Valley. The forest roads, north-east over Rievaulx Moor to East Moors and downhill to **Cowhouse Bank Wood**, connect with the Forestry Commission car park at *612 888*: a walk of $4\frac{1}{2}$ miles with someone to drive round to meet you is an attractive possibility; but nothing is laid out – you may find that stimulating. Take a map (OS 1:50,000 sheet 100), and compass.

NEAR YORK

Pleasant mixed conifer plantations north of Stamford Bridge at **Buttercrambe Moor**, *712 566*, offer possible walks in and out of woodland, especially in autumn when the fields are under stubble. The stubble is not burnt here but ploughed into the fine, dark soil. There are many wood and tree names about here; enough for a thesis. Buttercrambe means a 'cramp', bend or meander of the Derwent where butter was plentiful, (there is another crambe 6 miles downstream), or so the *Oxford Dictionary of Place Names* says. Clearly, this was a water meadow but Buttercrambe Ellers marks the site of elders near the river, while Stubbs Wood may have belonged to Stubbs or more likely was an oak coppice; woods are called Stubbs elsewhere in Yorkshire. Kissthorn Farm, to the north, must be on the site of a landmark thorn tree used as a trysting-place. West or east, old thorn trees were magic, though with subtle differences in the sort of magic they contained. There is a mysterious verbal link between 'witch' and 'quick' (with possible further links to 'wych'). Hawthorn is quickthorn because it is 'wick' – alive or lively, and this is a Yorkshire and Lincolnshire word. At least one eastern thorn tree, very ancient, was called a witch – the Witch of Hethel, near Norwich. As places have grown, old thorns, originally preserved out of superstition and becoming landmarks or meeting places, have been cleared away.

Nature reserves north of York are **The Moorlands** near Skelton, *580 587*, with a variety of exotic trees but best known for daffodils and rhododendrons – a charge is made in the flowering season – and **Strensall Common**, *653 618*, which is 94 acres of lowland heath with some birch scrub; army training ground to the south and adders on the heath. The reserve begins after the cattle grid on the Flaxton road out of Strensall village.

I have assumed that the Wolds are empty of woods, but don't be put off: there are good trees and shelter-belts in a landscape that is superbly clean-lined and free of visual atrocity.

HAWTHORN
Of the two native hawthorn's the quickthorn of the Inclosure hedges is *Crataegus monogyna*: the woodland hawthorn is *C. laevigata*. Together they must be our most common tree, but are not usually defined as trees for statistics. There are dense old coppices in our forests and acres of scrub on the Downs. In the north hawthorns often grow isolated by miles of moorland. May blossom is a symbol of fertility.

Bilsdale from Newgate Bank

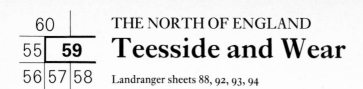
NORTH YORK MOORS (continued)

The northern part of the National Park is least forested but not the least handsome, and the silvery, distant array of industrial Teesside, Middlesbrough and Stockton does nothing to destroy the impressiveness of the great, angular shapes of the moors, here properly called the Cleveland Hills. The Forestry Commission as usual helps out with car parks, here serving the long-distance footpaths.

Clay Bank *573 035 viewpoint and 579 039, open moors, walks indefinite, FC*
The first of these is a viewpoint on the B1257 looking north; fine, but much excelled by a similar position 300 feet higher, reached by the expenditure of a little energy. The Lyke Wake

Walk section of the Cleveland Way here staggers between boulders, heavily eroded, before setting off eastwards for the treeless rigours of Farndale Moor and Rosedale Moor. West of the road the long-distance path at least looks over woodland and sometimes even enters it. The second car park is downhill amongst the trees.

Another Forestry Commission car park is above Great Ayton, *592 110*, **Gribdale Gate**, on the Cleveland Way about ½ mile from Captain Cook's monument, which challenges another, older landmark; the nipple-shaped Roseberry Topping. The hills here enclose the peaceful bowl of the Ingleby Beck.

North-north-west, now enmeshed in the network of Middlesbrough's outskirts, the little oasis of **Ormesby Hall**, *530 168*, remains lovely and is now preserved by the National Trust, with graceful but narrow perimeter woodlands. Great elms are gone from the park,

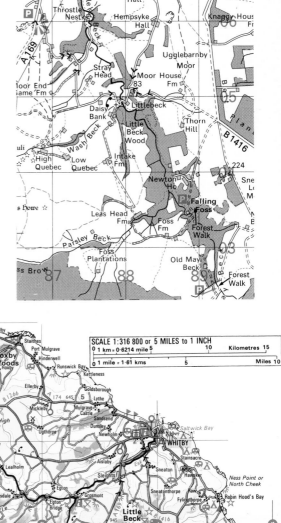

The Lyke Wake Path from above Clay Bank

as is the traditional cedar from the lawn by the grey, elegant hall.

Also within the North Yorkshire Moors National Park, to the north, is **Little Beck Wood**, a nature reserve of 32 acres; oak, ash, hazel and alder, *880 050* (park at Littlebeck Institute). The road here is quite remarkably steep. In **Roxby Woods**, *755 168*, inland from Staithes, the road is on a knife-edge of a ridge with a tree-filled valley on each side: turn off the A174 for Dalehouse and fork right immediately after the bridge; or approach from Scaling, by the reservoir on the A171, *744 128*. There is a picnic place at the east end of the reservoir.

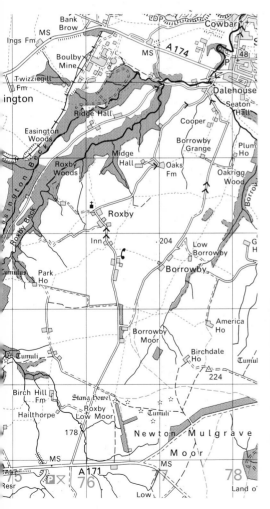

There is little else to satisfy Teesside tree-lovers until, westwards, south and north of Barnard Castle, are two great lungs of forestry.

The Stang *023 075*, ♀ , *1500 acres, 1m walk, FC*
The switchback road from Barnard Castle eventually climbs to a little car park at 1600 feet, through picturesque groupings of various evergreens which contrast with cleared and replanted areas and even larger areas of blanket bog. There is said to be a good view, but visibility was reduced when I visited. A lovely wild place – but bitterly cold in the mist.

Hamsterley Forest *093 314*, ♀ ♠ , *4800 acres, forest drive and walks, FC*
Aim for Bedburn from Hamsterley village. There was no toll point and the drive appeared to be open. It is not very impressive, in a rather dark valley, but it has its moments. Six forest walks are based on the eastern and western ends of the drive. I had the impression that hardly anyone visits Hamsterley, and indeed, perhaps only because of the peculiar dank mist and cloud at the time, I found it hard to like. It may be that the conifers sit too heavily in the deep dale; on a brilliant day it may well be fascinating. Still, with such a large area of softwoods, a little bit more elbow room for native trees in the valley would be more cheering. Admittedly it was planted with conifers as well as beeches long before the

Ink-cap fungus and spruces, Hamsterley Forest

81

The Stang

ALDER

It was coppiced for clog-makers – the wood is waterproof and lightweight. Now alders retain riverbanks. Once the woods were widespread; cleared, they left rich soil, often used for meadows, because the tree produces its own nitrogen from a symbiotic bacterium in the roots. The bark was used for tanning and also for dyes, and produced medicines, vomative when fresh, purgative dried. Altogether it has been a useful tree.

Forestry Commission took over.

Witton-le-Wear has a nature reserve at **Low Barns**, *161 316*, 84 acres: gravel workings, lakes and a mature alderwood. Access is limited to the nature trail, signposted ¾ mile east of Witton. There is a leaflet. The warden lives on the reserve; Witton-le-Wear 559.

On the coast between Peterlee and Seaham is **Hawthorn Dene**, *433 456*, a nature reserve of 165 acres which includes woods with snowdrops, described as spectacular, hawthorn scrub, and badgers. The road north of Hawthorn is signposted 'Quarry Traffic'; ½ mile along it is a gate to the reserve.

Castle Eden Dene, *410 387*, is a 300-acre mixed woodland in the long, narrow valley or ravine, on limestone and clay, with a network of paths. There is a fine larch plantation: alder and bird cherry by the burn. The nature reserve is run by Peterlee town council.

THE NORTH OF ENGLAND
Kielder Forest and
Tyneside Landranger sheets 80, 81, 87

THE BORDER FOREST PARK

One hundred and fifty-eight thousand acres or 245 square miles of once bleak and empty moorlands, where hardly a tree was to be seen half a century ago, are now Britain's largest forest. Even H. L. Edlin of the Forestry Commission, writing in 1958, admitted that there was 'a certain sameness about our Border spruce forests'. You have been at the Forest Centre at Kielder Castle only ten minutes before you are told that the forest is beautiful. It is a strange beauty; the visitor is more likely to react immediately to the immensity of the forest. On a clear day it really does look quite stupendous, as ridge after ridge of the hills reveal the dark, dense cover of even-aged conifers.

All the Border hills were once naturally forested with oak, alder, birch and pine, but centuries of grazing by deer, cattle and sheep, while the trees were gradually removed, reduced the land to grass – which first grew well in the woodland humus, then, gradually, exposed to the direct action of the weather, began to form peat. Eventually even the Cheviot sheep could not find sufficient to bite on and the moorlands, wild and remote, became a desert. Planting was begun at Smales in 1923, with Sitka and Norway spruce. At first each acre had 1750 turves cut by hand and a seedling planted in each inverted square, but from about 1940 various large-calibre ploughs were being used. By 1950 thinnings were already being extracted at the rate of 3 tons per acre. About 1500 men are now employed in the Border forests. They and their families live in gleaming villages which would make the best-kept southern village look quite a mess. The forest *is* beautiful, but it is almost the man-

Bakethin Reservoir, Kielder Forest

83

made beauty of a new, very efficient, machine.

The English part of the Border Forest Park consists of the Wark, Redesdale and Kielder Forests, covering 125,000 acres (including 45,000 acres of peaty hilltops and grazing). The area is rich in ancient historical remains.

Kielder Forest: Kielder Castle 633 935, ⚑, *Visitors' Centre, FC*

The centre is reached via the North Tyne Valley road and the new forest road from Bellingham, or by the B6357 to Scotland,

turning off at Saughtree. Kielder Castle is comfortably occupied by the Forestry Commission and is not generally open to the public. The Visitors' Centre has exhibition panels and a bookstall, a picnic place and a play area. There is a café, and wheelchairs can be accommodated. With so many trees in its control, it is a pity that the Forestry Commission could not manage a few to shade the parking ground.

Forest walks of 1½ miles, 2 miles or 5 miles start from here. A Forest Drive is in effect a

toll road east to Blakehopeburnhaugh on the A68 – there are several picnic places on the way with short waymarked walks.

There is a campsite, Class B with D-type toilets, 100 yards north of Kielder village, and another at Leaplish, 5 miles south. There are several picnic places around Kielder Reservoir, and a wildlife observation hide on Kielder Burn. You can fish on 2 miles of the North Tyne River, permits and bookings (none for the campsite) from the Chief Forester, Kielder Castle.

Wark Forest has a campsite at Stonehaugh and a picnic place, Warksburn, *790 762*, among tall spruces where there are three waymarked walks.

Falstone Forest, a Forestry Commission name for the bit connecting Kielder, Redesdale and Wark, has a picnic place at Sidwood, *777 890*, by Tarset Burn; turn off the so-called C200, or North Tyne road, to Greenhaugh.

Acorn Rigg Moss, *690 790*, is a National Nature Reserve within the Northumberland National Park: 88 acres of blanket bog at over

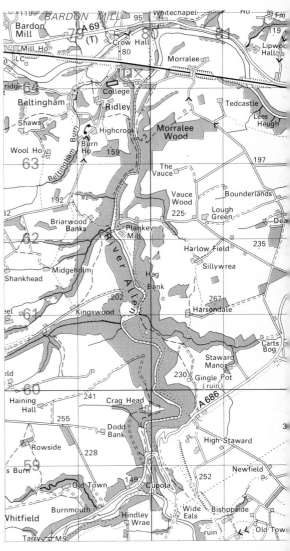

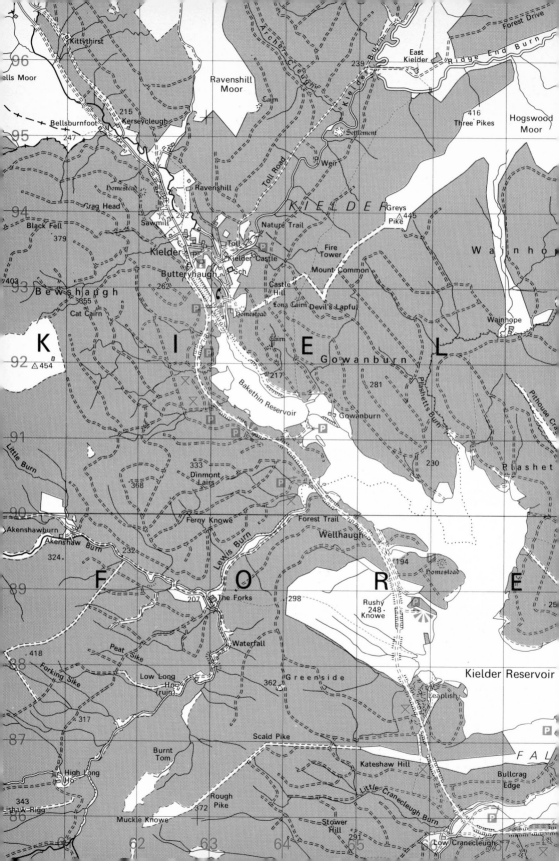

1000 feet with no history of human interference, says James Fisher. The Forestry Commission shares control, and perhaps provides the 'woodland' interest here.

SOUTH-EAST OF THE WALL

Allen Banks *797 643*, ♀ ♣ , *riverside walks, NT, NR*

South of the Roman wall in pretty Allendale the National Trust has 193 acres and the promise of much more. The very respectable parking place is made out of the kitchen garden of Ridley Hall, and has a map indicating walks in riverside woodlands (mixed, estate woods) of about 2 miles or less. Suspension bridges carry the footpaths across the river.

Briarwood Banks is a 29-acre nature reserve near Plankey Mill on the west bank of the Kingswood Burn before it joins the Allen; *796 622*. This is claimed to be the best fragment of ancient woodland in the Allen Valley. Cross a suspension bridge over the Allen and a small

bridge over the burn. It was raining very hard, and I had lunch instead, so it's all yours.

Tony's Patch *820 654*, ♀ , *4 acres, NR*

Anthony Clissold led three expeditions to Iceland in search of whooper swans before drowning at the early age of 37 in a local reservoir. This tiny but wild wood is his

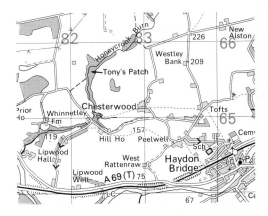

Elm in Tony's Patch

Northumberland roadside ash

memorial: healthy elms, with a wide range of other native trees, oak dominant, but only just, and a rich field layer. The minor roads here are narrow and some are, perhaps correctly, labelled 'No Through Road', so you must follow the directions exactly. Turn north off the A69(T) $1\frac{1}{2}$ miles west of Haydon Bridge, up a small road by a cottage advertising B & B. Turn left by a T junction after 1 mile, and look for a ladder stile $\frac{1}{2}$ mile on the right. Follow the fence to the wood by the Honeycrook Burn.

Plessey Woods, *240 799*, is a 60-acre Country Park, with fishing as well as woodland, near Bedlington. Gateshead has a wood, a nature reserve of 48 acres at **Thornley Wood**, *185 612*, in a valley with oaks and conifers.

An ash-tree drive

Nearly 20 miles of ashes line the rolling road from Walwick, north of Hexham, along the A6079 and B6342 to Rothbury. At first there are some sycamores, but then the ash trees continue in unbroken lines, only giving out when the road becomes straighter and the Harwood Forest appears on your left.

Before this, **Wallington Hall** (National Trust), *028 845*, is a really beautiful house and park; the park is richly planted with a variety of good trees, with many a sheltered seat by the walks. The woods are open always. Round about are no less than 12,970 acres of Trust lands, including Cambo village.

Nearer to Rothbury, a picnic place, *037 996*, is signposted '2 miles west', and this is a popular Forestry Commission stopping place close to the hills of Simonside – it can also be reached by a minor road from Rothbury, through Great Tosson. I had to select, and I selected wrong. The result was a sunny September afternoon spent in the malodorous shade of a vast rhododendron thicket at Cragside.

Wallington Hall

OPPOSITE: Cragside

North Northumberland
and Coquet Valley Landranger sheets 80, 81

Cragside, Rothbury *067 032 (entrance off B6341) (♀) ⚲, CP, drive, walks, NT*
The house was designed mainly by Norman Shaw, and finished in the 1890s for Sir William Armstrong, inventor and armaments king. It was the first house in the world to be lit by electricity from water power (and is probably the only one to have a hydraulic spit in the kitchen). Mature conifers in the policies are very impressive, and there are tall beeches too as you drive along, expecting somewhere to park. But you would be wise to park by the house and walk along the drive for there is little in store for you, except rhododendron. The seven parking places which constitute the Country Park element here are all attractive enough, especially the one called Crozier on a bare rock platform with heather in the cracks – but the walks are merely jungle tracks through the heavily overgrown *Rhododendron ponticum* varied by patches of *Gaultheria shallon* (the first plant described by David Douglas as soon as he landed in north-west America).

There are some very impressive large firs and Douglas firs by the lower lake, but you can hardly step back to see them. The upper lakes supplying the hydroelectric system are quiet places for birds, including heron, with moorland beyond, young pine and larch and, a final irony, pylons.

Holystone Burn *942 020* and **Holystone North Wood** *945 028, ♀, 93 acres, NR*
West out of Rothbury through Thropton and Sharperton are more roadside ash trees, here glittering against the yellow morning and evening skies which seem to be characteristic of the cold beauty of this nearly perfect countryside surrounded by smooth, bluish hills. At Holystone is a well, associated first with St Ninian and now with the National Trust. A little further west is a Forestry Commission car park among spruces, grassy and fungusy; and indicated on a notice-board map are the old oaks of Holystone North Wood. There is no particular path in the nature reserve and the going is tough through bracken; easy in mossy, grassy sections. The sessile oaks, over 38 acres, are varied in habit, some straight, some old coppice trees, some obviously once exposed. Now they are sheltered by the Forestry Commission spruces. One misses, therefore, the sense of being enclosed in a native wood: only at the top of the slope is an open patch where the oak trees stop and heather, with a patch or two of birch, takes over. There are also rowans. This would be a good wood to explore in the winter when the bracken is down – you may then be glad of the shelter of the conifers.

Various Forestry Commission waymarked walks take in the forestry plantations.

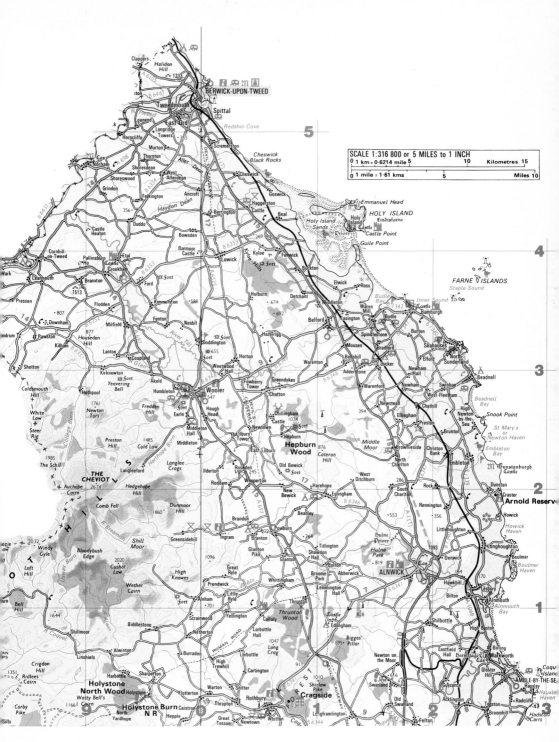

SCALE 1:316 800 or 5 MILES to 1 INCH

Oak and bracken in Holystone North Wood

The road (footpath) to the Holystone Burn

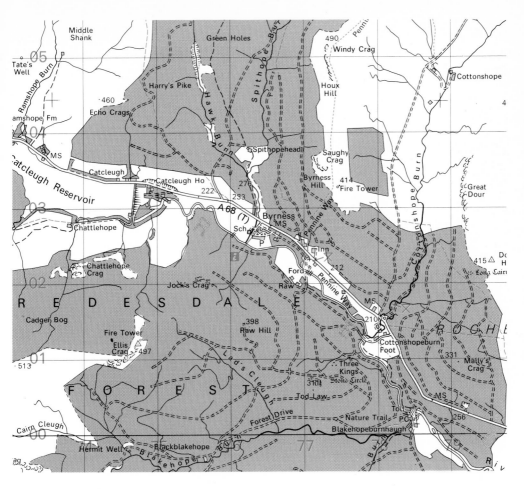

Drive up the Ministry of Defence private road, or walk if you prefer, to a lay-by with a fine view – where a forest road forks away about a mile from Holystone. Downhill from here is the Holystone Burn Nature Reserve with native trees which include juniper and oak, with bog myrtle. The army range is beyond the reserve.

The **Northumberland National Park** is largely of moorland and is shared with the Ministry of Defence, who often have a lot of red flags flying. Maps are placed at suitable access or non-access points, but intending explorers should seek guidance from the Information Centre at Rothbury, where Forestry Commission leaflets for up to a dozen different walks are also available.

Redesdale Forest (offices at Byrness) has three picnic places on or near the A68(T), and trout fishing on a mile of the River Rede.

Hepburn Wood, *075 245*, near Chillingham Park (with its famous herd) south-east of Wooler, has a Forestry Commission picnic place and three waymarked walks.

The **Arnold Reserve** at Craster is an old whinstone quarry with 3 acres of scrub and trees: *255 197*.

93

Index